Zen Mind, Thinker's Mind

New Perspectives on Buddhadharma, Consciousness, and Awakening

L. Ron Gardner

VERNAL POINT
PUBLISHING

CONTENTS

Introduction

In 2018, I decided that my next writing project would be a Buddhist "trilogy" consisting of texts on Dzogchen, Zen, and Pali Buddhism. I was motivated to undertake this project because I believe that Buddhism is in need of an "upgrade." As I see it, there isn't a single living Buddhism teacher-writer who has "cracked the code" and is thus able to properly elaborate on Buddhadharma, Consciousness, and Awakening. Given my view of the "fallen state" of Buddhism and my belief in my ability to "resurrect" it, I began my project.

I started my "trilogy" with the Dzogchen text, but at the point I was half-done writing it, a series of epiphanies convinced me to put it aside and instead focus on this Zen text. The gist of my epiphanies was that Zen, principally due to the influence of Madhyamaka, epitomizes the downfall of Buddhadharma; therefore, it deserved my first attention. Further, because Zen disses the thinking mind, I realized that it was most important from the outset of my project to counter its anti-mind ideology; hence the title *Zen Mind, Thinker's Mind*.

The book consists of sixteen chapters, which I'll now summarize:

Chapter 1. "Mind and No-Mind": Sheds light on the usage and meaning of the terms Mind, mind, no-mind, Awareness, and awareness, which are often used loosely, contradictorily, and/or synonymously by Buddhists.

Chapter 2. "The Emptiness of Emptiness": Considers Nagarjuna's doctrine of emptiness and concludes that his "Middle Way" is not a middle way at all, but rather, an extreme way that, egregiously, reduces Ultimate Reality (the Divine Existent) to a non-existent emptiness.

Chapter 3. "The *Tetralemma* and the Two Truths": Critiques the *tetralemma* (the four-cornered system of argumentation often applied in Buddhism) and the doctrine of the Two Truths (conventional and ultimate), and finds them untenable.

Chapter 4. "Light on the *Lankavatara Sutra*": Provides a ground-breaking explication and elaboration of the text's more abstruse teachings.

Chapter 5. "Ken Wilber's *Fourth Turning*": Critiques Wilber's thesis on the Turnings of the Wheel (especially the "Fourth Turning"), and provides an alternative vision (of Five Turnings) based on my Electrical Spiritual Paradigm (ESP).

Chapter 6. "Sam Harris on Waking Up": Exposes Harris's ignorance regarding religion and spirituality, and identifies him as a clueless mystic and an overrated thinker.

Chapter 7. "Dark Buddhism": Critiques Morgan D. Rosenberg's book *Dark Buddhism: Integrating Zen Buddhism and Objectivism*, and provides an alternative vision of "Dark Buddhism."

Chapter 8. "Zen Mind, Non-Thinker's Mind": Provides arguments and evidence to counter Third Zen Patriarch Seng Ts'an's famous saying: "Stop talking, stop thinking, and there is nothing you will not understand." The subchapters of this chapter are excerpted from my book *Beyond the Power of Now*.

Chapter 9. "Buddhist Politics 501": Argues that left-wing politics (socialism/statism), which most Buddhists favor, is violent and immoral, and that right-wing politics (capitalism/individualism) is non-violent and moral, and therefore the right politics for Buddhists.

Chapter 10. "Electrical Flesh, Electrical Bones": Argues that Zen needs to convert to Electrical "religion," and advances a brief theory of Electrical en-Light-enment. This chapter is excerpted from my book *Electrical Christianity*.

Chapter 11. "Who Am I?": Considers Self-enquiry (finding out who one truly is) in the contexts of current and mid-twentieth-century Buddhist teachings, and concludes with an in-depth analysis of Self-enquiry that is unparalleled in Buddhist literature.

Chapter 12. "Some Sayings of Huang Po": Provides commentary on some of iconic Zen Master Huang Po's most enlightening sayings.

Chapter 13. "The Sword of Thusness": Contends that there is just a single direct means or "method" to Enlightenment—that of Thusness, or Beingness—and elaborates it in the context of some sayings of Huang Po.

Chapter 14. "The Five Ranks of Master Tozan": Provides unique interpretations of the five stanzas that comprise ninth-century Zen master Tozan Ryokan's poem *The Five Ranks*, which describes the stages of Enlightenment in the practice of Zen.

Chapter 15. "Zen and Dzogchen": Compares Zen and Dzogchen and explains how Zen can benefit by incorporating Dzogchen's view and essential practices.

Chapter 16: "Future Zen": Consists of talks between a few of my students and myself, some of which recapitulate (while expanding upon) subject matter in the previous chapters, and some of which break new ground.

Because this book contains considerable Buddhist and Hindu terminology, I have included an extensive glossary. As with my previous nonfiction books, I have included my Spiritual Reading List, which I've upgraded with new additions.

The late, great Suzuki Roshi canonized the importance of the "beginner's mind" in Zen. It is my hope that this book will do the same for the "thinker's mind."

Notes to the Reader

Except for a handful of terms that have entered the common lexicon (such as yoga, tantra, mantra, guru, and karma), I have generally, but not in all cases, italicized Buddhist and Hindu yogic terms. One of the toughest tasks in writing spiritual books is deciding which terms to capitalize and when. For example, a term such as "Power" might merit capitalization in one context, but not another. The calls regarding italicization and capitalization were often subjective, and if I ever do a second edition, I'll doubtless end up changing some of them.

Throughout this book, you'll see references to texts with the directive "see my review" in parentheses. At the time I began this book, all of these reviews were available at Amazon. But Amazon, unceremoniously and sans a given reason beyond "violation of community standards," deleted my 300-plus spiritual book reviews. In response, I have posted all the reviews referenced in this book at my blog electricalspirituality.com, where they are available under the tab "Book Reviews." And they are also available in my just published Kindle ebook *Buddhist Book Reviews for Smarties*, which includes all my 100-plus Buddhist book reviews, and the non-Buddhist ones, referenced in this book.

In reading this book, you'll see that I sometimes capitalize "En-Light-enment" and sometimes don't. In general (though not always), when you see "En-Light-enment" (or "Enlighten-ment"), I am referring to full or final spiritual Awakening; and when you see "en-Light-enment," I am signifying the process of Awakening via Light-Energy. In borderline cases, where the term could apply to both the process of Awakening and final Awakening, I made a subjective call based on the context in which the term was used.

CHAPTER ONE

Mind and No-Mind

There is nothing in Buddhism more confusing than the usage and meaning of the terms Mind, mind, no-mind, Awareness, and awareness, which are often used loosely, contradictorily, and/or synonymously. It would take a book to properly consider this subject, but in the confines of a couple-thousand-word article, I'll attempt to shed some light on these terms by briefly elaborating them.

Mind

When "Mind" is capitalized, it should mean universal, transcendental Mind, or Consciousness, or Awareness. This Mind, in Sanskrit, is *Cit*. This unborn, unmanifest Mind, which never enters creation, is a synonym for Ultimate Reality.

In his Introduction to the *Lankavatara Sutra*, D.T. Suzuki writes:

> 'Mind-only' means absolute mind, to be distinguished from an empirical mind which is the subject of psychological study. When it begins with a capital letter, it is the ultimate reality on which the entire world of individual objects depends for its value. To realize this truth is the aim of the Buddhist life.

The *Lankavatara Sutra* states:

> I say there is nothing but Mind. It is not existence, nor non-existence; it is indeed beyond both existence and non-existence... Out of Mind spring innumerable things, conditioned by discrimination (i.e. classification) and habit-energy; these things people accept as an external world... What appears to be external does not exist in reality; it is indeed Mind that is seen as multiplicity, the body, property, and abode—all these, I say, are nothing but Mind.

The great Zen master Huang Po, in accordance with the *Lanka*, says:

> Only awake to the One Mind and there is nothing whatsoever to be attained. This is the real Buddha. The Buddha and all sentient beings are the One Mind and nothing else.

Mind, or the One Mind, has become everything; hence it is the True Nature of all existents. When a Zen student awakens to his Buddha-nature, he realizes Mind as indwelling; when he recognizes all existents as manifestations of Mind, he realizes Mind as universal.

The real problem is that many Zen writers, unlike John Blofeld in *The Zen Teaching of Huang Po*, don't capitalize Mind, which creates confusion between the finite, discursive "mind" and the infinite, non-discursive "Mind."

Mind is Consciousness, is Awareness, is the *Dharmakaya*. Mind, immanently (or in the context of a human), is Buddha, is Self, is *Nirmanakaya*. Mind as *Cit* (or pure Consciousness) should not be conflated with mind as *manas* (general mental activity). Mind is Buddha, mind is not.

In Buddhist literature (especially that of non-Cittamatra Yogacara), one sometimes reads that the world is a projection of one's mind. This is absurd, because the world is still there when your mind isn't. If you fell over dead in front of your computer, your computer would still be there for others sans you and your mind. Cittamatra (a sub-system of Yogacara) has it right: the world is a manifestation of Mind; hence everything, including one's mind, is (or derives from) Mind.

The mind

The mind consists of mental formations. When these formations are organized to function as discriminating intelligence, this, in Hindu yogic parlance, is referred to as *buddhi* (intellect, or "higher mind"). Just as *manas* should not be conflated with Mind (or Buddha), neither should *buddhi*. *Buddha* (or immanent Mind) is awakened Awareness, or Consciousness, in the context of an individual; *buddhi* is the function of "knowing" via mental formations.

In the Pali Nikayas (the Buddhist texts of the *Sutta Pittaka*), three terms—*manas*, *vijnana*, and *citta*—are used to refer to the mind. *Manas*, described in Patanjali's *Yoga Sutras* as the mind that processes and mediates sensory information and habit-tendencies (*vasanas*), means the same in Pali Buddhism. It is the general thinking faculty, or so-called "lower mind."

Vijnana, the fifth of the five *skandhas* (or empty-of-Self aggregates), is generally translated as "consciousness," and because it is, many Buddhists ignorantly assume that the Buddha rejected consciousness (or Consciousness) itself as non-Self. In reality, *vijnana* is not consciousness itself, but consciousness functioning as discrimination of the components and aspects of objects. Because *vijnana* is the dualistic (or subject-object) functioning of consciousness that creates the separate-self sense, it leads to suffering. As such, it is akin to the seventh consciousness (of eight) in Yogacara, sometimes (improperly in my view) termed *manas,* and sometimes (properly in my view) termed *klista-manas,* which identifies it as the self-grasping, and thus taint-ridden, mind. (See Chapter Four, "Light on the *Lankavatara Sutra,*" for more on this.)

According to Wikipedia, "The *Pali-English Dictionary* suggests *citta* is heart/mind, emphasizing it as the more emotive side of mind, as opposed to *manas* as the intellect in the sense of what grasps mental objects." The *Pali-English Dictionary* has it wrong. *Citta* is Consciousness itself (*Cit*) intertwined with *manas* and contracted by grasping (or acts of binding attention) engendered by *vijnana.* It is a synonym for the *Alaya-vijnana,* which is the *Alaya* (universal Consciousness) conjoined with *manas* by *vijnana* in the Heart-center/cave, the *Tathagatagarbha.* The locus of the immanent *Alaya* (*Cit,* or Mind) is felt-experienced two digits to the right of the center of the chest by advanced yogis. And it is here, in the Heart-center, where the "storehouse" of karmic seeds (*bijas* that "sprout" into *vasanas*), is located. When, through the Grace of *Dharmamegha* (the full-blown descent of the *Sambhogakaya*, which severs the Heart-knot), *Cit* is forever freed, so is *citta*, meaning *Cit* in relation with *manas*. In other words, in the Mind of a Buddha, mind (meaning thoughts) still arises, but because the binding (or self-contracting) function of *vijnana* has been rendered defunct, *citta* now unobstructedly reflects (or shines as) *Cit*, while still allowing for the function of thinking. This freed *citta* is *Bodhicitta*, signifying that the *bodhisattva* has been fully Awakened, or En-Light-ened, by the Light-Energy of the *Sambhogakaya*, which is realized in the *Tathagatagarbha* as inseparable from the *Dharmakaya* (Mind, or *Alaya*, or *Cit*).

The Enlightened State of *Bodhicitta* represents the "conversion" of the *Alaya-vijnana* (or *citta*) from a self-contracting "storehouse" consciousness into the immanent *Alaya* (or *Cit*), no longer bound by *vijnana-skandha* (discriminating mind). The Nature of *citta*, when "converted" to *Cit* in a human bodymind, is to shine, and when the self-contraction is obviated, *citta* radiates as luminous Mind. Per Wikipedia:

> Luminous mind (also, "brightly shining mind," "brightly shining citta") (Sanskrit *prakṛti-prabhāsvara-citta*, Pali *pabhassara citta*) is a term attributed to the Buddha in the Nikayas... In the Anguttara Nikaya (A.I.8-10) the Buddha states: "Luminous, monks, is the mind. And it is defiled by incoming defilements." The discourses indicate that the mind's natural radiance can be made manifest by meditation.

No-mind

The Zennist website (zennist.typepad.com) glosses:

> In the treatise On No-Mind attributed to Bodhidharma the
> term no-mind is never meant nor intended to leave us with
> the impression that no-mind is against direct intuition or
> awakening to something transcendent. A more pithy mean-
> ing for no-mind is "no discriminating mind." Such a no dis-
> criminating mind is the same as True Mind. In fact the trea-
> tise says: "Indeed, no-mind is nothing other than true mind.
> And true mind is nothing other than no-mind." Further on
> the treatise says: "What is called no-mind is nothing other
> than a mind free from deluded thought."

In contrast to the Zennist, I say that a no-discriminating mind is
not the same as True Mind. When one's mind is still, True Mind
does not suddenly appear in its stead. True Mind is Heart-Mind,
the transformed *Alaya-vijnana* that is free from bondage to all
conditioned consciousnesses. But this freedom from conditioned consciousnesses does not occur until one experiences the
descent of the *Sambhogakaya* into the *Tathagatagarbha*, the Heart-
cave, or "womb of Buddhahood." It's as if the Light-Energy of
the *Sambhogakaya* (a.k.a. *Shakti*, or the Holy Spirit) ignites *citta*
(immanent and contracted *Cit*, or Heart-Mind) and allows it to
shine as luminous Consciousness, or True Mind. A still mind, or
no mind, is a precursor to realizing True Mind, because it leads
to or instigates the descent of the *Sambhogakaya*. But prior to the
downpoured *Sambhogakaya* conjoining *citta*, True Mind cannot
be experienced. And upon the full and unobstructed descent of

the *Sambhogakaya* into the *Tathagatagarbha*, which produces the *samadhi*, or state, the *Lankavatara Sutra* calls *Dharmamegha*, the *bodhisattva* attains *Bodhicitta* and becomes a *Tathagata*, one who abides permanently in, and as, Suchness (or Being-Consciousness, or True Mind as it IS).

Zen Buddhism fails to explain how the experience of no-mind leads to the realization of Mind. If it explained this, that would also explain gradual and sudden Enlightenment. I'll now explain what Zen doesn't. When the no-mind state instigates the descent of the *Sambhogakaya*, the disciple, over time, experiences progressively more intense, or fuller, *samadhis* (which the Buddha termed *jhanas*). The experience of these *samadhis*, or *jhanas*, constitutes gradual Enlightenment. This experience does not pertain just to the freeing and intensification of consciousness, but also to the literal divinization (or en-Light-enment) of the body that is concomitant with these states of consciousness. This divinization process is energetic and involves the opening of inner-body channels (*nadis*) via the force-flow of awakened consciousness (termed *Kundalini-Shakti* in Hindu yoga). When this force-flow of awakened consciousness (via the chief and ultimate *nadi*, termed *Amrita Nadi*), "descends" (or, more precisely, is "sucked" into) the *Tathagatagarbha* (*Hridayam*, or Heart-center, in Hindu yoga), which is the "seat" of *citta* (contracted Mind, or Consciousness), it, for a time, frees *citta*, allowing it to shine as *Cit*, or Mind. And when the Heart-knot (or Self-contraction), in a timeless, or "sudden," moment, is severed through the Power of *Shakti* (the *Sambhogakaya*), then Mind (Self, or Buddha) is forever freed—and so is the empirical mind, for whenever thereafter thoughts arise, they are outshone (and thus rendered non-binding) in the Light (or radiant Intensity) of Awakened, or True, Mind.

Awareness and awareness

Whereas the common synonym for the Absolute in Hinduism is "Consciousness," in Yogacara and Zen Buddhism it is "Mind," and in Dzogchen it is "awareness" or "Awareness." The problem with using "awareness" (uncapitalized) as a synonym for the Absolute is that all living animals are aware, but clearly, they are not Enlightened. When "awareness" is capitalized, then it is a fitting synonym for the Absolute; when it is uncapitalized, adding a descriptor such as "awakened" before it serves to differentiate it from generic awareness and to identify it as transcendental.

Animals, and most humans, are *unconsciously* aware. When a yogi practices awareness, he is being *consciously* aware, which, when it "produces" *Dharmamegha*, culminates in Awakened awareness, which is tantamount to unbroken Self-Awareness, or Buddha-Consciousness.

An argument against the existence of a nondual State of pure Consciousness (or Awareness) is sometimes made by those who claim that such a State is an impossibility, because consciousness (or awareness)-without-an-object violates the most fundamental of all laws, the law of contradiction. To this, I say that

Consciousness is biune, Self-Existing as Subject (Self-Aware-ness) and Object (Self-Radiance). Thus, through the medium of a yogi, pure Consciousness (or *Siva*) "knows," or recognizes, Itself via its own radiant Energy (or *Shakti*), which reflects It-self back to Itself. In Buddhist terms, the *Dharmakaya* (Aware-ness), through the agency of a yogi, beholds Itself via the *Sam-bhogakaya* (Light-Energy), which is always inseparable from It, and, in fact, is It, in the "Form" of a formless, mirror-like, Self-reflecting, Spirit-current.

CHAPTER TWO

The Emptiness of Emptiness

For a three-year period in my life—1974-1976—I was deeply into the *Prajnaparamita Sutras*. My spiritual practice during this period focused on two things: developing a mind that dwells upon nothing, and seeing all things as empty. But then, thanks to the teachings of Adi Da Samraj (then known as Bubba Free John), I had an epiphany: I realized that my attempts to develop a non-abiding mind and to negate phenomenal reality by imagining it as empty were simply forms of the avoidance of relationship (or whole-body communion with the Whole).

After my epiphany, I continued, for a few years, to randomly attend sittings at Zen groups, but I no longer had an interest in Zen philosophy and its apotheosis of emptiness. I basically forgot about the emptiness Dharma until 2003, when a friend introduced me to the teachings of Ayn Rand, which not only enlightened me on emptiness, but also inspired me to study academic texts on the subject by Buddhism professors. As I read these texts, which typically explain emptiness philosophy in the context of Nagarjuna's Madhyamaka, I further refined my consideration of the subject, and I knew it was just a matter of time until I wrote on it.

Ayn Rand on Emptiness

According to Ayn Rand's Objectivist epistemology, emptiness, like nothingness, is a non-existent with no ontological status, and those who grant it such status are guilty of what Rand calls "the reification of zero." Emptiness is simply a term that describes the absence of something in relation to some "thing," meaning an existent. There must first be a thing that can be described as empty before one can speak of emptiness. We can describe a coffee cup or one's head as empty, but once the cup is filled with coffee or one's head with knowledge, emptiness, a dependent quality, is vanished.

How about universal empty space? Surely that must be proof that emptiness is all-pervading and exists apart from, and even prior to, objects. Not true, I say. Although space is universal and formless, it is not empty, but teeming with sub-atomic particles and quantum activity. And the fact that scientists cannot create a vacuum devoid of subatomic particles proves that emptiness cannot be created.

What then is space if not emptiness? Along with many others, I contend that space is actually an ethereal substance, an emanated interface between the Unmanifest and the material world. And the fact that gravity curves space proves that it is substantial rather than empty. When so-called empty space is understood to be the ether, the *pranically*-charged, subtle-realm medium that lies between, and connects, the Divine Realm and the material world, then a proper theosophical understanding of the "structure" of the All is possible.

The *Heart Sutra*

The *Heart Sutra* is without doubt the most revered scripture in the Zen Buddhist canon. Regularly chanted before Zen sittings, it summarizes the fundamental Zennist view of reality. And the epitome of this view is made clear in the first two sentences of the *Sutra*, which go: "Form is not different from emptiness, and emptiness is not different than form. Form is emptiness and emptiness is form."

What's wrong with this Zennist view of reality? First off, if form is not different from emptiness, then why is there a need for an emptiness doctrine? Why not just have a form doctrine and reduce everything to form? Instead of seeing everything as empty, as Zennists do, why not just see everything as form? If an emptiness doctrine were central to spiritual life, then why don't all spiritual traditions have one? Among the Great Spiritual Traditions, only certain schools of Mahayana Buddhism apotheosize the void. If emptiness were Ultimate Reality, then Christianity, Hinduism, and Islam would also apotheosize the void; but they don't.

Real-world experience informs us that form and emptiness are not the same. Try walking through a wall in your room, and no matter how hard you try to convince yourself that form and emptiness are the same, your experience will tell you otherwise. How then can we make sense of the *Heart Sutra*? By understanding it as a provisional teaching that, by reducing form to emptiness, fosters non-attachment to the material world.

As such, its function is the same as the Hindu *Maya* doctrine, which enjoins yogis to see the world as unreal.

When singer-mystic Donovan, in his song *There is a Mountain*, rhapsodizes, "First there is a mountain, then there is no mountain, then there is," he's telling us that the ordinary man and the Zen master both see the mountain as a mountain, but that the Zen student, striving to become a master, negates the mountain by seeing it as empty. Again, this can be understood as a provisional practice, which the cognoscenti reject in favor of a more direct approach to Awakening.

What the *Heart Sutra* (and the *Prajnaparamita Sutras*) is really about is crossing to the Other Shore, which means Awakening as the Heart, one's Buddha-nature. *Prajnaparamita* (lit. the Perfection of Wisdom) means wisdom (or cognizant *citta*) that has crossed over, or gone beyond, *samsara*, and merged with *Bodhi*, meaning the awakening Light-Energy that "produces," or unveils, *Bodhicitta*, or Buddhahood. When it's understood what the *Heart Sutra* is really about, it's also understood what the emptiness doctrine is about.

Nagarjuna's Middle Way

Nagarjuna is probably the most important thinker in Buddhism after Gautama. Many Buddhists, including renowned integralist Ken Wilber, consider him a genius for the ages. I, however, am not one of the many. In fact, I contend that Nagarjuna's Madhyamaka (or "Middle Way") does not represent a "greater

vehicle" than Gautama's, but a lesser one. Nagarjuna's Madhyamaka philosophy can be summarized thus:

Everything—meaning all phenomena in all states—exists con-
ventionally, or nominally, or provisionally, but not inherently.
In other words, whatever exists, exists, or co-arises, interde-
pendently with other phenomena. This dependent co-arising,
or interconnected origination, is called "emptiness," because
it implies that whatever arises has no independent self-existence or self-nature; therefore its "essence" is emptiness. This
further implies that nothing, in and of itself, is born or dies,
or produced or annihilated. Hence the "extremes" of existence
and non-existence are negated, and what's left, according to
Nagarjuna, is the non-abiding Middle Way of emptiness, or
thusness, the "ultimate reality" of things.

The point of demonstrating this "emptiness" is to lead one
to Nirvana. But Nagarjuna's Nirvana is not Gautama's. In his
book *Nagarjuna's Seventy Stanzas*, author David Ross Komito,
who parrots Nagarjuna, writes:

> The emptiness of inherent existence of all phenomena is
> the naturally abiding nirvana which can be seen directly by
> a person on the Path of Seeing. Thus the term 'naturally
> abiding nirvana' and 'emptiness' are synonymous.

Nagarjuna doesn't have a clue what Nirvana is. Nirvana is
not a matter of seeing all existents as empty, as free from the
"extremes" of inherent existence and nihilistic non-existence.
Moreover, Nirvana cannot be "seen" because it is not an ob-

ject. *Nirvana*, as Gautama defines it, is the drying up of the outflows, the defilements that perpetuate *samsara* (or becoming). Nirvana is the end of becoming; therefore, it is Being, which, relative to a *bodhisattva*, is awakened timeless, spaceless Awareness. But because Nagarjuna was a deluded philosopher and not an awakened Buddha, he ignorantly reduces Nirvana to "emptiness," an emptiness or voidness, which, unlike in the case of Zen and Dzogchen masters, is not synonymous with an Absolute, or Mind, or *Dharmakaya*.

Nagarjuna is right when he says there has never been a single thing, but he is wrong in failing to identify all "pseudo-entities," or conventional existents, as derivative modifications or permutations of a single Great Existent, or all-subsuming Being, or Mind. Nagarjuna's "emptiness" is not the Ultimate Reality of all things; Consciousness-Energy, the Divine Being, is. By failing to identify timeless Awareness as the *Dharmadhatu*, the all-pervading, spaceless Substratum underlying phenomenal existence, Nagarjuna is guilty of "Context-dropping."

In India, Shankara, figuratively speaking, "kicked Nagarjuna's butt" in debates by making it clear that *Brahman*, not emptiness, is the Condition of all conditions, and that true Nirvana is Self-realization. Moreover, Yogacara's "Mind-Only" Buddhism, which arose in India, also rejected Nagarjuna's metaphysics, as it emphasized Mind, not emptiness, as the Essence of all phenomena.

But today, Nagarjuna's nonsense lives on, as modern-day Prasangika-Madhyamaka Buddhism professors, such as Jeffrey

Hopkins, Guy Newman, and Jay Garfield continue to push his "Middle Way" as the apex of Buddhist thought.

For example, in his book *The Fundamental Wisdom of the Middle Way*, Professor Garfield, a la Nagarjuna, rejects the importance of essence and identity. According to Garfield, "It is important that objects and their characteristics, personas and their states be unified. But if we introduce essence and entity into our ontology this will be impossible."

In diametrical opposition to Professor Garfield, I say that unless we introduce Essence (timeless Awareness) and Entity (the Divine Being, or Adi-Buddha, or *Trikaya*, or Godhead, or the Unborn and Unmade of Gautama) into our ontology, this unification, and a consequent integral philosophy, is impossible, because contrary to what Nagarjuna and Garfield preach, all *dharmas* are not empty. Rather, they are temporary non-binding modifications or permutations of Mind-Energy, the Radiant Transcendental Light-Consciousness; hence, in agreement with modern physics, and in contradistinction to Nagarjuna, all things are not reducible to emptiness, but to Energy, which itself is irreducible. Ultimate Reality is not dependent origination and the emptiness or essencelessness of all phenomena; it is Self-Existing, Self-Energetic Self-Awareness. And this is Self-evident to an Awakened, or En-Light-ened, One.

If you read Garfield's book, you will find that Nagarjuna cannot write clearly, that he specializes in cryptic passages that are difficult to decipher. You will also find that he makes ridiculous statements. For example, even Garfield has to reject his absurd statement "The identity of mover and motion; the agent and action are identical." Here are a few more examples of his defective thinking:

> Compound phenomena are all deceptive. Therefore they are false. Whatever is deceptive is false.

Unbeknownst to Nagarjuna, phenomena are neither true nor false, nor deceptive nor non-deceptive; they just are. The categories that Nagarjuna superimposes on phenomena are simply his own biased and deluded concepts.

> Whatever is dependently arisen, such a thing is essentially peaceful. Therefore, that which is arising itself are [sic] themselves peaceful.

Again, Nagarjuna is guilty of superimposing his own value-judgments on phenomena. According to his "logic," even Hiroshima was "peaceful."

> It is not tenable for that which depends on something else to be different from it.

In other words, if you depend on food stamps, you're not different from them. If you depend on the sun's light, you're not different from the sun. What self-evident nonsense.

What Nagarjuna attempts to do in his discourse is to demonstrate the emptiness of all phenomenal existents, including conditions, effects, elements, aggregates, et al. The end result, in Garfield's words, is: "As far as analysis, one finds only dependence, relativity, and emptiness, and their dependence, relativity, and emptiness." Beyond informing us ad nauseum that everything under the sun is dependently originated, and thereby, necessarily, essenceless or empty, Nagarjuna, a circumscribed thinker, has virtually nothing to say.

The Buddha didn't find what Nagarjuna found, mere emptiness. He found the "Uncompounded, the Unmade, the Unborn." And rest in this unmanifest, timeless, spaceless Domain, the *Dharmakaya*, is *Nirvana*, the end of *samsara,* the succession of time-bound, unsatisfactory states of being. But Nagarjuna, a pointy-headed philosopher, just like Jay Garfield (birds of a feather flock together), never moves beyond the analysis of phenomena to a recognition of the Reality that underlies conditional appearances. Whereas Nagarjuna and Garfield repeatedly encounter infinite regresses, the great sages encounter real Emptiness, the Great Void—formless, timeless, spaceless Awareness, or Mind, the hypercosmic Substratum that eludes Nagarjuna, who can't fathom a Supreme Source prior to and beyond phenomena.

If you are interested in Nagarjuna's disintegral "fishbowl" philosophy, with lengthy Indo-Tibetan interpretations by a hyper-intellectual academic seemingly incapable of moving beyond the confines of Prasangika-Madhyamaka and into real Spirituality—Mind (the *Dharmakaya*) and Energy (the *Sambhogakaya*) and the direct means to realize them—then Garfield's book could be for you.

If, on the other hand, you are interested in an impressive, inexpensive text by an author who, like me, finds Nagarjuna an affront to Aristotelian logic, then you might want to get philosophy professor Avi Sion's *Buddhist Illogic: A Critical Analysis of Nagarjuna's Arguments*. Here is Sion's description of the text:

> [The text] demonstrates the many sophistries involved in Nagarjuna's arguments. Nagarjuna uses double standards, applying or ignoring the Laws of thought and other norms as convenient to his goals; he manipulates his readers, by giving seemingly logical forms (like the dilemma) to his discourse, while in fact engaged in non-sequiturs or appealing to doubtful premises; he plays with words, relying on unclear terminology, misleading equivocations, and unfair fixations of meaning; and he 'steals concepts,' using them to deny the very percepts on which they are based.

In summary, I contend that Nagarjuna's Middle Way is a perversion of original Buddhism, and that Nagarjuna was to Gautama what Joseph Smith and John Calvin were to Jesus—a perverter of the religion's original Teaching. I contend that his "Middle Way" is not a middle way at all, but rather an extreme way that, egregiously, reduces Ultimate Reality (the Divine Existent) to a non-existent emptiness.

CHAPTER THREE

The *Tetralemma* and the Two Truths

[This is a redacted conversation between a student of mine and myself. In our discussion, we first consider the *catuskoti,* the four-cornered logico-epistemological system of argumentation commonly referred to as the *tetralemma* in Buddhism. This system, which is antithetical to Aristotle's three "Laws of Thought," seeks to invalidate the identity of all *dharmas* (existents) and to negate all views as a means to attaining Nirvana. We then consider the Buddhist doctrine of the Two Truths (conventional and ultimate) and how it can be reconfigured to redefine Mahayana's "Middle Way."]

The *Tetralemma* and Aristotle's Laws of Thought

Jan Westerhoff, a prominent professor of Buddhist philosophy, writes: "The Indian philosopher Acarya Nagarjuna (c. 150-250 CE) was the founder of the Madhyamaka (Middle Path) school of Mahayana Buddhism and arguably the most influential Buddhist thinker after Buddha himself. Indeed, in the Tibetan and East Asian traditions, Nagarjuna is often referred to as the 'second Buddha.'" But you reject Nagarjuna's status as the "second Buddha," and instead designate

him as the principal subverter / perverter of Gautama's original Bud-
dhism. Can you elaborate the basis of your disdain for Nagarjuna?

Yes, I consider Nagarjuna to be to Buddhism what Im-
manuel Kant is to Western philosophy: the arch-enemy
of reason (in relation to reality) and the principal figure in
its attack on man's consciousness and conceptual faculty. And
rather than being an Enlightened Buddha, or *Tathagata*, he was
merely a second-rate philosopher who specialized in sophistry,
contradictions, and illogic.

Let's first consider Aristotle's three "Laws of Thought," which
we can summarize as: "A is A" (Identity), "Nothing is both
A and non-A" (Non-contradiction), and "Nothing is neither
A nor non-A" (Exclusion of the Middle). These laws are not
mere hypotheses, but incontrovertible axioms. To deny their
validity is to deny the identity of existents and man's cognitive ability to identify these existents and the properties
they entail. Logic is the non-contradictory identification of
reality (or the facts of reality), and because Nagarjuna denies
identity, and therefore the validity of identification, he is an
enemy of logic.

Now let's consider the *tetralemma*, a device that describes the
four possible stances to a proposition (P):

1. P (affirmation)

2. Not P (negation)

3. Both P and not P (both affirmation and negation)

4. Neither P and not P (neither affirmation nor negation)

Nagarjuna applies the *tetralemma* to negate the four ontological "extremes," or "limits":

All things (*dharmas*) exist: affirmation of being, negation of nonbeing

All things (*dharmas*) do not exist: affirmation of nonbeing, negation of being

All things (*dharmas*) both exist and do not exist: both affirmation and negation

All things (*dharmas*) neither exist nor do not exist: neither affirmation nor negation

By rejecting these four alternatives (affirmation, negation, double affirmation, double negation), Nagarjuna rejects all firm standpoints and instead points to a "middle path" between being and nonbeing. This "middle path" is typically described as a path between the "extremes" of essentialism and nihilism, but because no such middle exists, and because existence, identity, and hence knowledge (which is dependent on identification) are negated by it, this path is itself nihilism. And the eighth-century Hindu sage Adi Shankara, who defeated Madhyamaka opponents in debates across India (precipitating Buddhism's decline in that country), identified it as such.

Besides being guilty of violating Aristotle's Laws of Thought and preaching the very nihilism his so-called Middle Way rejects as an "extreme," where else does Nagarjuna fail?

A book could be written on this subject, and philosophy professor Avi Sion has already written one—*Buddhist illogic: A Critical Analysis of Nagarjuna's Arguments*—which impressively dissects and criticizes Nagarjuna's philosophy. So rather than rehash his analysis, I will simply recommend his book for those interested in an academic consideration of Nagarjuna's faulty logic and epistemology.

But beyond Nagarjuna's faulty logic and epistemology is his untenable metaphysics, which Sion, a non-mystic, cannot properly consider. In short, Nagarjuna fails to identify an Ultimate Reality—call it Mind, or *Dharmakaya*—that transcends self-existence and non-existence. Instead, for him, Ultimate Reality, or Nirvana, is simply the recognition of all *dharmas* as empty, meaning devoid of self-essence or intrinsic nature (*svabhava*). Because even emptiness itself is empty to Nagarjuna, his "middle path" culminates in an "extreme," or totally reductionist, "realization" of Ultimate Reality as merely the recognition of the "non-reality," or insubstantiality, of phenomenal existence.

Great Zen masters, on the other hand, point to a single Existent, or universal Mind, as Ultimate Reality. And because this Mind, or Being-Consciousness, is immanent as well as transcendent, they also refer to it as *Buddha.* To the cognoscenti, it is obvious that Mind is an analogue for God, *Siva*, or *Brahman*, while *Buddha* is one for Christ, Self, or *Atman*. And because this Ultimate Reality is formless, Zen masters also refer to it as the Void, or Great Emptiness. But in contrast to the empty emptiness of Nagarjuna, this "Emptiness" is full of Mind, or Consciousness.

The Two Truths Doctrine and the "Middle Way"

I'm interested in your take on the Two Truths doctrine in relation to Madhyamaka. Here [below] is Wikipedia's description of this doctrine:

> The Buddhist doctrine of the two truths differentiates between two levels of *satya* (A Sanskrit and Pali word meaning truth or reality) in the teaching of the Buddha: the "conventional" or "provisional" (*saṁvṛti*) truth, and the "ultimate" (*paramārtha*) truth.
>
> The exact meaning varies between the various Buddhist schools and traditions. The best-known interpretation is from the Madhyamaka school of Mahayana Buddhism, whose founder was Nagarjuna. For Nagarjuna, the two truths are *epistemological truths*. The phenomenal world is accorded a provisional existence. The character of the phenomenal world is declared to be neither real nor unreal, but logically indeterminable. Ultimately, phenomena are empty (*sunyata*) of an inherent self or essence, but exist depending on other phenomena.

Again, Nagarjuna misses the mark. If he had been spiritually awake, he would have advanced a Three Truth doctrine that integrates the "conventional," the "provisional," and the "ultimate." The "conventional" truth perceives phenomenal objects as possessing *svabhava*, meaning independent own-being; the "provisional" truth perceives these objects as being "empty," meaning lacking *svabhava*; and the "ultimate" truth perceives Mind as the only reality, meaning that all phenomenal objects are manifest forms of unmanifest Being-Consciousness.

So, Nagarjuna not only errs by conflating rather than contrasting "conventional" and "provisional" truth, as you define the terms, he also errs by reducing "ultimate" truth to "provisional" truth.

Yes. First, the Zen student sees a mountain as a mountain, which is "conventional" truth. Then, he "sees" the mountain as empty, which is "provisional" truth. Lastly, upon Enlightenment, he sees the mountain as both a mountain and a manifestation of Mind. And this spontaneous, unbroken recognition of all existents, including oneself, as Mind is "ultimate" truth. But for Nagarjuna, who views "ultimate truth" as the non-existence of Ultimate Truth, meaning Mind, or Being-Consciousness, there is only "conventional" truth and "provisional" truth (which is no more than a remedial method to counter "conventional" truth by imagining all existents as empty).

So, there is only one Truth?

As Huang Po puts it, "There has never been a single thing... There is only the One Mind, beside which nothing exists." But even though all existents are but forms of the single Existent, or Being-Consciousness, for us to function in the "real," or conditional, world, we, as conditional beings, must also acknowledge the truth (or reality) of its laws, distinctions, and boundaries.

But if there is only the One Mind, or Being-Consciousness, which has become everything, doesn't that negate individual identity and result in the same nihilism as Nagarjuna's Madhyamaka?

No. Once the One Mind, or "God," emanates the universe of existents from Itself, creating the phenomenal worlds, a.k.a. *Maya*, these existents are endowed with individual identities. Moreover, the One Mind, or "God," has blessed man with the cognitive ability to identify, and thus differentiate, these existents.

So, in *Maya*, that which has been measured out from the Immeasurable, a.k.a. "God," or Mind, individual things and beings are a reality; but from the viewpoint of the Absolute, there has "never been a single thing," because all "things" are simply temporary manifestations of the "Thing Itself," the One Mind, or Being-Consciousness.

So, from this perspective, the Two Truths are the "absolute," or "nondual," truth (meaning there is only God), and the "conditional," or "dual," truth (meaning there is not only God, but also separate existents with individual identities). But if you find that it serves your spiritual practice to imagine entities as empty, then feel free to include this third, or "provisional," truth.

CHAPTER FOUR

Light on the *Lankavatara Sutra*

The *Lankavatara Sutra* (abbreviated LS or *Lanka*) is a profound and important Mahayana Buddhist sutra. It propounds the doctrine of Cittamatra, a sub-system of Yogacara which asserts that a single universal Mind (or Consciousness) has become everything. As such, the LS is akin to Hindu Kashmir Shaivism and Tibetan Dzogchen, which likewise assert that a single omnipresent Consciousness or Awareness (*Siva*, or *Dharmakaya*) has manifested as all existents.

Unfortunately, however, if an impressive LS commentary has been penned since D. T. Suzuki's in his *Studies in the Lankavatara Sutra* and *The Lankavatara Sutra* in the early 1930s, I haven't encountered it. What separates Suzuki's analysis from those of other LS exegetes is his understanding of LS's Cittamatra philosophy. Unlike other authors on the said subject, he groks the important distinctions between the Yogacara Cittamatra of the LS and the Yogacara Vijnaptimatra of Asanga, Vasubandu, and others. Most importantly, he understands that, per the LS, all existents are manifestations of a universal Mind, and not projections of one's individual mind, as other Yogacara schools have it.

Suzuki makes the important point that the LS does not represent an end point in the development of Yogacara philosophy,
but rather a transitional one. For example, he informs us that
"the Trikaya is not yet systematized in the *Lankavatara Sutra*."
Regarding the LS's stage of development, he writes:

> The *Lankavatara Sutra* is not a systematized treatise devoted
> to the exposition of a definite set of doctrines, but a mine
> containing all assorts of metals still in the state of requiring
> analysis and synthesis. It is full of suggestive thought which
> must have been fermenting at the time in Mahayana think-
> ers' minds and hearts. The two great schools of Mahayana
> Buddhism, the Madhyamaka and the Yogacara, lie here in an
> incipient stage of development and differentiation.

Just as the LS does not represent a final stage in the evolution
of Yogacara, likewise Suzuki's exegesis of the *Lankavatara Sutra*
does not represent the final word on the LS—and Suzuki himself would be the first to admit this. So, while Suzuki's writings
are must-reading for those seriously interested in the LS, they
are far from comprehensive or definitive, hence there is much
that can be said to further explicate and elaborate the *Sutra*'s
teachings. With this in mind, I'm moved to provide my own
exegesis of some of the LS's more abstruse teachings.

Descent into Lanka

To the spiritual cognoscenti, it is clear that the LS is about
the descent of the Divine (as the *Dharmamegha*, or "Dharma
Cloud") into the *Tathagatagarba* (or Heart-cave), which precip-

itates full Enlightenment, or *Bodhicitta*. The term "Lankavatara" means "descent into Lanka," and Lanka (a solitary, or sacred, "island," like Sri (meaning "Holy") Lanka, is a metaphor for the *Tathagatagarbha*, the "place," or "locus," or "womb," where one is "reborn" as a Buddha. In the Hindu *Yoga Sutras*, reaching this "island," (a.k.a. *Hridayam*, or Heart-center) is termed *kaivalya*, which means "isolation" from the defilements that, in Yogacara terms, taint the seven forms of consciousness that precede the en-Light-ening eighth one, *Alaya-vijnana*. Yogacara means "the practice of yoga," and the highest yoga, Di-"vine" yoga, is the union of the "vine" of the Dharma Cloud (or *Shakti*, or *Sambhogakaya*, or Clear-Light Energy, or Holy Spirit, or Mother Light) with the "vine" of the yogi's consciousness (or *citta*, or soul, or son light) in the Heart-cave (or *Tathagatagarbha*). This union results in the severing of the Heart-knot (which Gautama called the Heart-release), thereby permanently disentangling one's Self (or Buddha-nature) from the defilements of the first seven forms of un-en-Light-ened consciousness.

Who or What descends into Lanka to en-Light-en the *bodhisattva* (the en-Light-enment-seeking disciple)? The *Bhagavan* (Red Pine's term in his text *The Lankavatara Sutra: Translation and Commentary*), which D.T. Suzuki, in his translation of the *Lankavatara Sutra*, translates as the "Blessed One." The *Bhagavan*, or Blessed One, as Blessing Power (the *Sambhogakaya*, or Clear-Light Energy, or Dharma Cloud, or *Shakti*) does. On the first page of Chapter One, Red Pine writes, "The Bhagavan had been expounding the dharma for seven days in the palace of Sagara, the Serpent

King."The seven days represent the seven forms of consciousness prior to the en-Light-ening eighth. Sagara is one of eight serpent kings who acted as protector of the Dharma (really, protector of the realization of the *Dharmakaya*). Sagara's residence was at the bottom of the ocean, which is analogous to the *Tathagatagarbha*, the irreducible root of Consciousness in a human. Sagara, the eighth Serpent King, represents the Heart (or Gordian)-knot, the final guardian of the Gate to the *Dharmakaya*. The Serpent King is another name for *Kundalini*, the "Coiled One"—and when the final, Heart "coil" is "straightened" by the Blessing Power (or Clear-Light Energy) of the Blessed One, then the *bodhisattva* morphs into a Buddha, a *Tathagata* who dwells time-lessly in, and as, the *Dharmakaya*, universal Mind, or Awareness.

Mind Versus mind

The real problem with contemporary scholars who write on the LS is that they have no grasp of Yogacara's Mind-Only (Cittamatra) Dharma. For example, in the first paragraph of Chapter One in his book *Lankavatara Sutra: Translation and Commentary*, Red Pine translates a sentence in the *Sutra* as follows: "[Bodhisattvas] skilled in the knowledge that external objects are perceptions of one's own mind..." Contrast this with D.T. Suzuki's translation: "The Bodhisattva-Mahâsattvas... all well understood the significance of the objective world as the manifestation of their own Mind."

Unbeknownst to Red Pine, Mind (the *Alaya*, the Unborn Substratum) is a metaphysical "Substance," and the world is the objectification, or manifestation, of this Mind. This point of view, called Cittamatra (or Consciousness-only), is in diametrical opposition to Red Pine's point of view, called Vijnaptimatra (or mind-only), which sees the world as nothing but ideas, with no Reality or realities behind them, and which reduces all *dharmas* (or things) to mere mental projections, or representations, of one's individual mind. External objects, however, are not, as Red Pine asserts, perceptions of one's own mind. If you believe that the computer you're using now wouldn't exist just as it is after you stopped perceiving it, then you have evicted yourself from reality.

Red Pine doesn't understand that universal, transcendental Mind (with a big "M"), the unmanifest *Alaya*, or *Dharmakaya*, has manifested as the universe of existents. In other words, the *Alaya*, which is Mind-"Substance," has modified itself as stepped-down vibrations of energy and matter into the totality of phenomena. And his gross and egregious misunderstanding effectively destroys his entire analysis of the *Lankavatara Sutra*, rendering it essentially worthless. Red Pine has read Buddhist scholars such as Florin Sutton (author of *Existence and Enlightenment in the Lankavatara Sutra*) and Dan Lusthaus (see my review of his *Buddhist Phenomenology*), and these so-called "experts" on Yogacara have doubtless infected his brain with their exoteric, non-spiritual, psychologized interpretations of the Mind-Only teaching.

The viewpoint that Mind, the *Alaya*, or *Dharmakaya*, has become everything is hardly heterodox (even though modern Buddhist scholars reject it). It is the same one espoused by

Zen masters Hui Neng and Huang Po, Yogacara masters Saraha and Padmasambhava, Dzogchen master Longchen Rabjam,
and numerous others. Here's a quote from Saraha, from *Prin-
cipalYogacara Texts* (see my review):

> Thus know that the whole appearance is the Dharmakaya. All
> sentient beings are the Buddha. All cosmic arisings and events
> are from the beginning not other than the Source of Phenom-
> ena (Dharmadhatu). For this reason, everything that one can
> identify conceptually is as unreal as are the horns on a rabbit.

The Eight Consciousnesses

According to the excellent Wikipedia.org article "Eight Consciousnesses":

> All surviving schools of Buddhist thought accept – "in
> common" – the existence of the first six primary con-
> sciousnesses (Sanskrit: *vijñāna*). The internally coher-
> ent *Yogācāra* school associated with Maitreya, Asaṅga,
> and Vasubandhu, however, uniquely – or "uncommon-
> ly"– also posits the existence of two additional primary
> consciousnesses, *kliṣṭamanas* and *ālayavijñāna*, in order to
> explain the workings of *karma*. The first six of these pri-
> mary consciousnesses comprise the five sensory faculties
> together with mental consciousness, which is counted as
> the sixth.

The first five consciousnesses—eye, ear, tongue, nose, and
body—pertain to the senses, and the sixth consciousness, *ma-*

no-vijnana, is the mental consciousness that cognitively processes the sense-data and engages in concept formation.

The seventh consciousness, termed *manas* or *klista-manas*, is
deluded awareness, one's consciousness beset by *klesas* (mental afflictions or disturbing emotions). The root cause of the
klesas is the self-contraction, the formation of awareness into a
separate-self sense that, to one degree or another, is suffering.
In reaction to this constricted separate-self sense, craving for
experience arises in an attempt to heal the dis-ease that the
contraction engenders. But it never touches the contraction;
at best, it provides only brief desensitization to it in the forms
of fascination, consolation, and distraction. After a craving is
satisfied, another, and then another, arises as the self-contract-
ed individual is caught in a vicious cycle of becoming (*samsara*),
as he goes from one (limited, and thus unsatisfactory) state
of consciousness to another, all the while not recognizing his
activity as a reaction to the contraction.

Klista-manas is the self-reflecting, self-reifying, self-seeking
activity of the separate self in dilemma. As such, it is akin to
the *ahamkara* in Patanjali's *Yoga Sutras*. Because *klista-manas*, as
self-reflection, includes the capacity to analyze and judge, when
confronted with the truth about itself (as self-contraction), it
can then apply its discriminating intelligence (akin to *buddhi* in
the *Yoga Sutras*) to the ordeal of obviating the self-contraction.

The eighth consciousness, *Alaya-vijana*, must be understood
from two perspectives: the unenlightened (meaning prior to

Enlightenment) and the Enlightened (meaning after Enlightenment). Before a *bodhisattva* attains *Bodhicitta*, full Enlightenment, the *Alaya-vijnana* functions as a storehouse consciousness that contains the karmic seeds (*bijas*), or subconscious mental impressions (*samskaras*), which concatenate into *vasanas* (habit-energies or behavioral tendencies), which, in response to internal and external stimuli, transmute into mind in the form of *mano-vijnana and klista-manas*. After a *bodhisattva's* full Enlightenment, when his karmic seeds have been "fried," meaning rendered non-binding, the *Alaya-vijnana* functions as the immanent *Alaya* (the Unborn Realm, or Universal Mind). As such, the term *Alaya-vijnana* is somewhat misleading, because in the case of a Buddha, *vijnana*, which implies divided or dualistic consciousness, no longer implicates him in *samsara*.

The "Jungianization" of Yogacara

The *Lankavatara Sutra* is the most authoritative and influential text of the Yogacara (or "Mind-Only") school of Indian Mahayana Buddhism, but it is a deep and abstruse work—and this has led to very different interpretations of its core tenets pertaining to the True Nature of Mind (or Consciousness). And in his text *Existence and Enlightenment*, author Florin Sutton (a professor of Asian studies) argues, as his core thesis, that

> Universal Consciousness [or Mind] is best understood as the consciousness which is common to all men, and, in this sense, universal (i.e., the subconscious in its most basic or pure state, the '*Alaya*'), rather than some universally pres-

ent 'stuff,' 'entity,' or 'substance,' existing independently outside the realm of human mental activity.

From my perspective, Dr. Sutton, couldn't be more wrong regarding universal Consciousness, the *Alaya*. Universal Consciousness is the universal, transcendental "Mind-Stuff," the unmanifest "All" that has manifested as the "all" (the universe of existents), but yet is utterly and forever independent of its manifestation.

Sutton's misunderstanding of Yogacara is hardly limited to the *Alaya* and the *Tathagatagarbha*; it extends into other areas of Buddhadharma as well. For example, a chapter in his book is entitled "Dharmadhatu; the Spacial or Cosmic Dimension of Being." Unbeknownst to Sutton, the *Dharmadhatu* is not a cosmic dimension or space; it is the acosmic *Dharmakaya* as the spaceless "context" in which phenomena arise.

Sutton not only has a problem understanding Yogacara, he also seems to lack even a rudimentary understanding of Hinduism. For example, he defines the *Atman* as the "empirical Self." Anyone with a clue about Hinduism knows that the *Atman* is the metempirical (or transcendental) Self, not the empirical (or phenomenal) Self.

If modern Buddhism scholars, such as Dr. Sutton, bothered to study Hindu yoga philosophy, they would understand the various schools of Buddhism from a more nuanced, more integral perspective. But, unfortunately, most of them are married to a viewpoint that precludes the consideration of Buddhadharma in a spiritual context that extends beyond the boundaries of Buddhism.

The LS as a Hybrid

The *Lankavatara Sutra* is not a "pure" and systematized treatise, but a hybrid or mishmash that reflects distinctive elements from three different schools: Yogacara, Madhyamaka, and the classical yoga of Patanjali. Hence, if you want to understand the LS, you not only need to study Yogacara and Madhyamaka, but also Patanjali. And the text I recommend for this is *Yoga Philosophy of Patanjali* by Swami Hariharananda Aranya. To those who have studied Patanjali and Advaita Vedanta, it is obvious that the Mind that the Blessed One (or *Bhagavan*, or Buddha) discourses on in the LS is the same metaphysical "Substance" as the Self (or *Atman*). In fact, throughout this quasi-Hinduized text, awakening to, and as, Mind is equated to Self-realization, which is a synonym for Nirvana, or Buddhahood.

The *Lankavatara Sutra* is not an easy, amenable read. It is, as Buddhist scholar Edward Conze puts it, "an unwieldy system of viewpoints, paths, and categories, explained in difficult technical terminology." It is convoluted, repetitious, replete with contradictions, and flies off on speculative metaphysical tangents that have no bearing on the central theme of Mind-realization. A major reason for the contradictions is that the text is the work of more than one author, at different times. For example, as D.T. Suzuki points out, the section against meat eating is clearly a later addition to the root text, and was added to mitigate criticism against Buddhism for condoning flesh consumption.

A major problem with this text is that it briefly mentions, but fails to elaborate and integrate, essential elements of the Buddhahood project, such as baptism and the *Dharmamegha* (or Dharma Cloud). A couple of times in the text, the Blessed One, in a sentence, mentions Buddhas baptizing *bodhisattvas*, but nothing more is said, and no details are provided, about this Spirit (or *Shakti*) transmission.

The Blessed One equates Mind-awakening with the tenth and final stage of Buddhahood, known as the Great *Dharmamegha*. This is likewise the final stage of Self-realization in Patanjali's yoga system; hence Buddhism coincides with Hindu yoga at this point.

What is the *Dharmamegha*? Although I'm no fan of the late Osho (Bhagwan Shree Rajneesh), he summarizes it nicely: "Dharmamegha means that the Self-nature has started showering you, and you yourself become bathed in it, drown in it."

In the *Lankavatara Sutra*, the Blessed one describes the *Bodhisattva*'s final stage thus: "Going through the successive stages of *Bodhisattvahood*, he finally reached the state of the Dharma Cloud [Dharmamegha]."

To the spiritual cognoscenti, the *Dharmamegha* (or Dharma Cloud) is the unobstructed descent of *Anugraha-Shakti*, the Holy Spirit, or *Sambhogakaya*, as the Blessing Power that transforms a *bodhisattva* into a Buddha, a Blessed One. When this Clear-Light Energy unites with contracted Mind, or *Siva* (*Alaya-vijnana*, or *citta*), in the *Tathagatagarbha* (the womb of the Buddhas, which is an analogue for the Hindu Heart-cave, or *Hridayam*), then Mind shines freely as *Bodhicitta*, or *Siva-Shakti*.

If you're interested in learning more about the energetic dimension of Awakening, which the LS briefly alludes to but doesn't elaborate (such as Buddhas baptizing *bodhisattvas*, and the *Dharmamegha*), I suggest checking out texts on Dzogchen, Hindu Kashmir Shaivism, Ramana Maharshi's esoteric teachings, and Adi Da's Daism. These texts will provide you with a "meta-view," so to speak, of the fragments of "pneumatology" found in the LS.

The LS and Zen

When Bodhidharma brought Chan Buddhism to China in the fifth or sixth century, his teachings centered on meditation and the *Lankavatara Sutra*. Of this, D.T. Suzuki, in his *Studies on the Lankavatara Sutra*, writes:

> The study of the *Lankavatara* may best be approached in its especial relation to the teaching and history of Zen Buddhism. It was principally due to Bodhidharma, father of the Zen in China, that the sutra came to be prominently taken notice of by students of Buddhism, and it was mainly by his followers that its study was systematically carried on and its commentaries written.

But due to the *Lankavatara*'s inaccessibility, its decline of influence in Zen was inevitable. Of this, Suzuki writes: "When even scholars of the first grade found the *Lankavatara* so hard to read, the natural result was to leave it alone on the shelf for the worms to feed on it." The coup de grace to the *Lankavatara's* influence in Zen occurred when the sixth patriarch of Zen, Hui Neng, figuratively anointed the *Diamond Sutra (Vajracchedika)* as the principal text of the tradition. Suzuki, in his *Studies on the Lankavatara Sutra*, provides an illuminating statement from Buddhist scholar Chiang Chih-chi on this transition of texts. He writes:

> The statement made by Chiang Chih-chi in his preface to the Chin-shan edition of the *Lankavatara* sheds light on the history of the sutra and also on the state of affairs in the Buddhist thought-world of his day (1085), and we give the following extract: "Of old when Bodhidharma was here from the West, he handed the mind-seal over to the second patriarch, Huik'e, and afterwards said: 'I have here the *Lankavatara* in four fasciculi which I now pass to you. It contains the essential teaching concerning the mind-ground of the Tathagata, by means of which you lead all sentient beings to open their eyes to the truth of Buddhism.'" According to this we know that Bodhidharma was not one sided, both the Buddhist sutra and Zen were handed over to his disciple, both the mystical and the letters were transmitted. At the time of the fifth patriarch, the *Lankavatara* was replaced by the *Vajracchedika* which was given to the sixth patriarch. When the latter [while peddling kindling wood] heard his customer recite the *Vajracchedika,* he asked him whence he got the text. He answered, "I come from Mt. Wu-tsu, east of Wang-mai, in

the province of Chin where Hung-jen the Great Master advises both monks and laymen to study the *Vajracchedika,* which will by itself lead them to an insight into the nature of being and thus to the attainment of Buddhahood." Thus the holding of the *Vajracchedika* started with the fifth patriarch, and this is how the sutra came into vogue and cut short the transmission of the *Lankavatara.*

This transition of texts signified the de-esotericization of Zen. According to prominent "Integral" philosopher Ken Wilber, when the *Diamond Sutra* displaced the *Lankavatara,* "Zen lost the philosophical and psychological sophistication of the Lankavatara system and focused almost exclusively on nonconceptual Awareness." The ramifications of this transition were (and are) far-reaching. Consequently, a significant amount the material in *Zen Mind, Thinker's Mind,* directly or indirectly, focuses on the effects of this transition.

CHAPTER FIVE

Ken Wilber's *The Fourth Turning*

K en Wilber is considered by many to be the world's greatest living philosopher. Wilber, who bills himself as a "pandit" (Dharma scholar/teacher), specializes in integral theory and solutions, which provides the lens through which he views humanity's past, present, and future. And in his 2015 book *The Fourth Turning: Imagining the Evolution of an Integral Buddhism*, Wilber focuses his "integral lens" on Buddhism (the religion he most vibes with), and envisages another (or Fourth) Turning of its Wheel that would embody the principles that are at the heart of his Integral philosophy.

In *The Fourth Turning's* Introduction, Wilber informs us that the world's religions "need to get serious about updating their fundamental dogmas." He says that the core ideas can be maintained but that new discoveries about spiritual experiences, spiritual intelligence, and spiritual development during the past thousand years need to be integrated into an Integral framework that includes and transcends the central teachings of the traditions. I agree with Wilber's goal but disagree with some of his ideas about the "upgrade," and I detail my disagreements in this article. Most importantly, I think Wilber misses the essence of what a new Turning of the Wheel should be about.

Wilber's book is arranged in three parts, with Part 1 focusing on Buddhism's past, Part 2 on its present, and Part 3 on its future. In Part 1, Wilber presents a brief history of Buddhism's essential past, meaning the Three (or Four) Turnings of the Wheel. According to Wilber, the First Turning, by the Buddha, represented "renunciation," the Second, by Madhyamaka, was about "transformation," and the Third, by Yogacara (and Vajrayana), introduced "transmutation." As Wilber points out, Vajrayana can also be viewed independently as the Fourth Turning.

In my opinion, Wilber doesn't grok what these Turnings are about because he doesn't deeply understand Buddhism or mysticism. I'll summarize what the Turnings are really about, then deconstruct Wilber's Buddhism and mysticism.

My Vision of the Four Turnings

I maintain that there have been Four Turnings of the Wheel in Buddhism: 1) The Buddha's original Dharma, 2) Madhyamaka's emptiness Dharma, 3) Yogacara's Mind-only (or Buddha-nature) Dharma, and 4) Vajrayana's tantra Dharma. And in contrast to Wilber, who only envisions spicing up Buddhadharma with elements of his Integral theory (mainly transpersonal developmental psychology and a sociopsychology of religion), I argue for a subsequent, or Fifth, Turning of the Wheel that would usher in a new school of Buddhism which demystifies the previous Turnings and incorporates their respective essences into a truly holistic new

Buddhadharma. I call this new school of Buddhism "Electrical Buddhism," and I do so because, as I'll explain, each of the Turnings after the Buddha's represents one-third of Ohm's Law.

The First Turning of the Wheel, by Gautama Buddha himself, set the Wheel in motion; the second, by Madhyamaka, emphasized emptiness (Absence, or "Ohms reduction"); the third, by Yogacara, accentuated Mind (Presence, or "Voltage"); and the fourth, by Vajrayana, focused on Energy (Power, or "Amperage"). The Fifth Turning would not only unify Buddhism, but also integrate it with Christianity; and I elaborate this theme in my book *Electrical Christianity: A Revolutionary Guide to Jesus' Teachings and Spiritual Enlightenment.*

I call the paradigm that integrates Ohm's Law with Christianity and Buddhism the Electrical Spiritual Paradigm (ESP), and I contend that this paradigm radically demystifies spiritual en-Light-enment. I'll now provide a summary of it in relation to the Three Turnings that followed Gautama's.

First, for those who are unfamiliar with Ohm's Law, it states that "the strength or intensity of an unvarying electric current is directly proportional to the electromotive force and inversely proportional to the resistance in a circuit." Ohm's Law—where V = voltage (electromotive force), I = amperage (intensity of current), and R = ohms (units of resistance)—can be summarized in three formulas:

$$V = IR; I = V/R; R = V/I$$

(Note: Any form of the Ohm's Law equation can be derived from the other two via simple algebra.)

Madhyamaka, the first of the three Turnings that followed Gautama's, emphasized emptiness, which equates to self-emptying, or Ohms (or resistance) reduction. Yogacara, the subsequent Turning, emphasized Mind, or Conscious Presence, which generates Consciousness-Force or Pressure, which is akin to Voltage (electromotive force). In electricity, electrical energy, or Amperage, is directly proportional to Voltage and inversely proportional to Ohms reduction; and Vajrayana Buddhism, which turned the Wheel after Yogacara, emphasized spiritual Energy, which is akin to Amperage. In short, each of the three Turnings after Gautama's represents one-third of the fundamental Law of Electricity—Ohm's Law.

Interestingly enough, some scientists argue that electromagnetism is the only fundamental force in the universe. Wilber talks about integrating modern science with Buddhadharma, and to my mind, where this integration should begin is by considering the Turnings of the Wheel in the context of electrical energy, specifically Ohm's Law.

Wilber's Vision of a Fourth Turning

Many imagine that Ken Wilber is an all-time great spiritual teacher. For example, Jim Marion, author of *Putting on the Mind of Christ*, describes Wilber as "one of the greatest and most brilliant spiritual teachers of all time." In contrast to Marion, I contend that Wilber is hardly the brilliant spiritual teacher or philosopher that many imagine him to be. With this in mind, I'll now point out some of the flaws in Wilber's understanding of Buddhadharma, and also Hindudharma.

First off, Wilber doesn't understand Emptiness, which he emphasizes in his exegesis of Madhyamaka and Yogacara. He conflates Emptiness with Ultimate Reality, which he also conflates with Nothingness. If he had studied Ayn Rand's Objectivism (which he pretends to have done), he'd realize that he's guilty of the reification of zero, attributing ontological status to a non-Existent. Nothingness does not exist, so form, or existents, cannot derive from it. Emptiness is likewise a non-Existent; it is simply a term to describe the absence of existents. Emptiness is a derivative, not the Great Ontological Primary. There must be Something to be empty, and that Something is Mind, or Consciousness. Unbeknownst to Wilber, Mind is empty, or formless, but it is not Emptiness; it is Consciousness. Emptiness is really about self-emptying, or self-nullification, which allows Consciousness-Force (Voltage) to transmute into a Light-Energy current (Amperage).

Wilber, in goose step with the *Heart Sutra*, tells us that Form is not different from Emptiness, and that Emptiness is not different from Form. If the two aren't different, then where is the need for an Emptiness doctrine? Wilber also tells us that Emptiness is a synonym for Suchness, or Thusness, or Isness. The Hindus, properly, laugh at this. According to them, Is-

ness, or Being (*Sat*) = Consciousness (*Siva*)-Spirit (*Shakti*). But
Wilber doesn't understand Being, which he reduces to Spirit,
which he conflates with Emptiness. Spirit is not emptiness; it is
the en-Light-ening Action, or Energy, of Being. Being is Con-
sciousness-Spirit, or Consciousness-Energy. Spirit, or Clear-
Light Energy, because it is perceived, is the "objective" side of
Being, while Consciousness, or Mind, because it perceives, is
the "subjective" side.

In addition to being ignorant of Emptiness, Suchness, and Spirit, Wilber doesn't grok the Buddhist *Trikaya* (*Dharmakaya, Sambhogakaya, Nirmanakaya*), which I contend is the same Triple
Body as the Christian Trinity (Father, Holy Spirit, Son). Wilber
tells us that the *Dharmakaya*, which is unborn Mind, or timeless Awareness, is synonymous with the Hindu Causal Body.
He's wrong, and if he understood Advaita Vedanta, he'd know
that the *Anandamaya Kosha*, the Bliss Sheath (the fifth of the five
sheaths that cover the Soul, or Self, or Buddha-nature), is the
Causal Body. The *Anandamaya Kosha*, or Bliss Sheath, is the same
Body, or Dimension, as the Buddhist Bliss (or Light-Energy)
Body, the *Sambhogakaya*, which, when contemplated dualistically rather than nondualistically, functions as a sheath, meaning
that it obstructs Self-realization. But Wilber tells us that the
Sambhogakaya is analogous to the Subtle Body. This is patently
false, because the *Sambhogakaya*, which is *uncreated* Clear-Light
Energy, is utterly distinct from the Subtle Body, which, in Advaita Vedanta parlance, consists of three *created* sheaths: the life-
force (*pranamaya kosha*), the lower-mental (*manomaya kosha*),

and the higher-mental (*vijnanamaya kosha*). In other words, the *acosmic Sambhogakaya*, which never enters spacetime—it is in it but not of it—should not be confused with the *cosmic* sheaths, or bodies, that constitute the Subtle Body.

Although Wilber's description of Yogacara Buddhism and its principal text, the *Lankavatara Sutra*, is less than "integral" (for example, he doesn't differentiate Cittamatra from Vijnaptimatra or mention the *Tathagatagarbha* or *Dharmamegha*), he, most importantly, does understand that when the *Diamond Sutra* displaced the *Lankavatara*, Zen lost its sophistication. He writes:

> *Lankavatara Sutra* was so important it was passed down to their successors by all 5 of the first Chan (or Zen) Head-Founders in China, as containing the essence of the Buddha's teachings. In fact, the early Chan school was often referred to as the Lankavatara school, and a history of this early period is entitled Records of the Lankavatara Masters. (Starting with the 6th Head-Founder, Hui Neng, the *Diamond Sutra*—a treatise solely devoted to pure Emptiness—displaced the *Lankavatara*, and in many ways Zen lost the philosophical and psychological sophistication of the Lankavatara system and focused almost exclusively on nonconceptual Awareness. Zen Masters were often depicted tearing up sutras, which really amounted to a rejection of the 2 Truths doctrine. This was unfortunate, in my opinion, because in doing so, Zen became less than a complete system, refusing to elaborate conventional maps and models. Zen became weak in relative truths, although it brilliantly succeeded in elaborating and practicing ultimate Truth.)

Wilber's vision for an Integral Zen and Buddhism, however, doesn't involve re-emphasizing the *Lankavatara*. Rather, it's about marrying his Integral philosophy with Buddhadharma. And in Part 2 of *The Fourth Turning*, he presents seven central ideas to achieve this union: 1) structures and structure-stages of development, 2) states and vantage points, 3) shadow and shadow work, 4) quadrants (four perspectives and dimensions that all phenomena possess), 5) typologies, 6) the miracle of "we," and 7) the impact of interior thinking.

I will now briefly critique these seven central ideas.

Structure-stages, the first of Wilber's central ideas, are the evolutionary philosophical "windows," or vantage points, through which people view and filter their life experiences, including what Wilber identifies as the four major states of humans: gross, subtle, causal, and nondual. From the lowest to the highest, these structures-stages, according to Wilber, are: archaic, magic, mythic, rational, pluralistic, integral, and super-integral. Humans can experience any of the four states from the vantage point of any of these stage-structures. According to Wilber, "structures are how we grow up and states are how we wake up."

I think that structure-stages provide a useful tool for understanding the various cultural mindsets throughout history; they explain how these mindsets have evolved while the four major states have remained the same. But just as Wilber doesn't understand the four major states very well, he likewise goes awry with his structure-stages hierarchy. His "integral" doesn't belong above "rational" because it is irrational, opposed to the political primacy of constitutional republicanism. Wilber, ignorantly and irrationally, equates individual freedom with representative democracy, which is a euphemism for majority mob rule, which empowers the (usually clueless) masses to vote away the rights and freedom of individuals. If Wilber had evolved to the (truly) rational level, he'd understand that the representative democracy he lauds is tantamount to "two wolves and a sheep deciding what they'll have for dinner." But because Wilber has not evolved to the (truly) rational level, he's unqualified to identify the structure-stages beyond rational; hence, his hierarchy falls apart and has no place in a Fourth Turning of the Wheel.

Wilber goes just as awry with his second central idea, states and vantage points, as he does with his first, structures and structure-stages of development. He emphasizes the importance of vantage points "in determining human experience [meaning states of consciousness]—how it is seen and how it is interpreted," but the vantage points he provides are flawed, because he doesn't deeply grok the Self-awakening project. He uses terms he doesn't understand—such as *Nirmanakaya*, *Sambhogakaya*, *Dharmakaya*, gross, subtle, causal, and Spirit—to explain dimensions and states of awakening; and rather than clarify the process, he muddles it. For example, he describes the ultimate state of nondual Awareness as "the union (and transcendence) of individual self and infinite Spirit." But he doesn't have a clue what Spirit is—Blessing/Blissing Clear-Light Energy, which is the same hypostasis as the *Sambhogakaya*, which he erroneously conflates with the subtle body. Because Wilber has been infected with what I call the "Madhyamaka virus," he thinks that Spirit is a synonym for emptiness, but as the cognoscenti know, emptiness is a non-existent with no ontological status, whereas Spirit is *Shakti*—Divine Power, or Light-Energy. But Wilber, sadly, has nothing to say about this Light-Energy in relation to the En-Light-enment, or Self-awakening, project.

Wilber's third central idea, shadow work to understand and deal with one's shadow, or "dark side" (which Wikipedia.org defines as "an unconscious aspect of the personality which the conscious ego does not identify itself"), is certainly a positive recommendation. Regarding the need for shadow work, Wilber writes:

> We know from long, hard, bitter experience in meditation from the time of its introduction in the West some 40 years ago, that meditation won't cure shadow issues and often inflames them. We all know meditation teachers who are often superb state teachers but structurally are shadow-ridden neurotic nuts, to put it as politely as I can. Don't be a victim of your own shadow, but include at least a little shadow work along with your meditation.

Wilber recommends and describes a couple of (what he terms 3-2-1 and 3-2-1-0) methods to address one's shadow problems. I find these methods, which are purely psychological, to be superficial. From my perspective, the first thing necessary to deal with one's shadow is right thinking, specifically right ethics (meaning the understanding of and adherence to the non-aggression principle). Right ethics prevents one's shadow, or "dark side," from infecting others, because an adherent to such ethics will not do things that infringe upon the rights, space, or sovereignty of others. But Wilber doesn't respect the non-aggression principle. In fact, the pluralistic (meaning liberal-authoritarian) politics he promulgates are diametrically opposed to it, as they promote the forceful enslavement of individuals by a Leviathan State and New World Order.

In addition to his 3-2-1 and 3-2-1-0 methods, Wilber also suggests psychotherapy as a means to deal with one's shadow issues. But better than psychotherapy for understanding one's shadow is astrology, for no other method can provide an objective map of one's root psychological tendencies and complexes. Once an individual understands his unconscious psychical "structures" and employs the non-aggression principal—not only in relation to others but also to himself—then no harm will come from his "dark side."

I have been to, and socialized with, Jungian psychoanalysts, and from personal experience, I can say that astrologers with an understanding of Jungian psychology are more effective than psychoanalysts in providing shadow analysis and counseling. Such astrologers can graphically describe a client's shadow elements, including their anima or animus. This is particularly important for male spiritual teachers, for it is their unregenerate anima which all too often precipitates their sexual misbehavior and downfall.

Although shadow work is important for self-understanding, it hardly qualifies as an essential component for what constitutes another Turning of the Wheel. But Wilber, whose goal is to impose his "Integral" vision on Buddhism, imagines that it does.

Wilber's fourth central idea involves integrating his four-quadrant model into Buddhism. This model, which consists of 1) Upper Left; interior-individual (intention), 2) Upper Right; exterior-individual (behavioral), 3) Lower Left; interior-collective (cultural), and 4) Lower Right; exterior-collective (social), reveals him as epistemically challenged. If he'd studied Ayn Rand's Objectivist epistemology instead of hanging his hat on Charles Peirce's Sign Theory, or Semiotic, he'd understand that his description of his four-quadrant model as "the four perspectives and dimensions that all phenomena possess" is nonsense. Human minds possess perspectives, phenomena don't. But Wilber isn't just epistemically challenged, he's also delusional regarding the importance of his four-quadrant model, which constitutes the core of his Integral philosophy. When he states that "The stages of meditation, in other words, like virtually everything else, are a four-quadrant affair," the cognoscenti can only laugh at his ignorance and hubris.

I second Wilber's fifth central idea, that of typologies—but he misses the boat with the typologies he designates as important in the creation of an Integral Buddhism. In my view, there can be no Integral psychology and no Integral Buddhism without astrology, a nonpareil tool for understanding self, others, and relationships on a karmic level. But Wilber, partially buried in the very zeitgeist "flatland" he heavily criticizes, fails to acknowledge astrology as a valid tool for self-other understanding. However, he buys into the Enneagram (a ninefold typology of personality types), which unbeknownst to him, derives from astrology, which subsumes and transcends it as a system of human classification and understanding. Wilber also acknowledges Myers-Briggs personality types as a means to self-understanding. The four fundamental personality types in Myers-Briggs—feeling, sensation, intuition, thinking—correlate closely with the four astrological elemental types—water, earth, fire, and air—and a professional astrologer, which I was for many years, can assess the "elemental" constitution of individuals far better than the Myers-Briggs test.

Wilber's sixth central idea, the miracle of "we," is hardly a new idea or ideal. In reality, it's just another attempt by Wilber to inject his four-quadrant model into Buddhism. Wilber writes, "But what is central for an Integral Spirituality is not that it focus merely on the collective 'We,' but that it integrate all 4 quadrants in each and every moment." As an example of a "miracle of 'we'" practice, Wilber cites Andrew Cohen's intersubjective yoga:

> Andrew Cohen recommended a type of "intersubjective yoga" (Lower Left Quadrant) where the individual lets go of self-identity and instead identifies with awareness itself (and "the ground of being") and especially the evolutionary impulse itself and its urgency, and then lets this evolutionary intelligence speak through every group member. When done correctly, this is often reported as feeling like a "group enlightenment."

If you want to know how successful Cohen's intersubjective yoga has been, Google "integral abuse: Andrew Cohen and the culture of evolutionary enlightenment." You'll find that it has not only been unsuccessful, but destructive. In short, a Fourth Turning of the Wheel would do well to skip on Wilber's miracle of "we" idea.

Wilber's seventh central idea, the impact of interior thinking, is no more than a plug for the application of his four-quadrant model to the process of reasoning. If you vibe with Wilber's left-wing "progressivism" and New World Order politics, you'll appreciate his model of integral interior thinking; but if, like me, you don't, then you'll categorically reject it and its inclusion in a Fourth Turning of the Wheel.

Part 3 of Wilber's book, "The Future," is simply a superfluous regurgitation, or summary, of Part 2. And speaking of summaries, here is mine of this book: It is simply Wilber's Integral Theory plastered on top of Buddhadharma. If you are already familiar with Wilber's Integral theory, you won't find much, if anything, new here. And Wilber is one of the last writers I'd recommend for anyone wanting to learn what Buddhadharma and mysticism are really about. In short, the "pandit" is in over his head when it comes to envisaging a Fourth Turning of the Wheel.

CHAPTER SIX

Sam Harris on Waking Up

Sam "Hardly a Sage" Harris

Many people consider Sam Harris to be a paragon of rationality and gnosis, an exemplar of enlightened post-postmodern wisdom who marries science and spirit. I don't. And in this article, I seek to expose Harris's ignorance regarding religion and spirituality. I aim to "behead" him with my "Dharma Sword" and expose him as an overrated thinker and a clueless mystic.

Harris is a philosophic "bottom-feeder" who specializes in pontificating on exoteric subjects with mass appeal. His books—most notably *Letter to a Christian Nation*, *The Moral Landscape*, *Free Will*, and *The End of Faith*—are geared to the common man who rejects conventional religion and seeks answers through science and reason.

Harris, however, doesn't just want to dis conventional religion—particularly Islam and Christianity—he also wants to be the "guru," or knowledgeable guide, who educates the common man about spiritual awakening. And his book *Waking Up: A Guide to Spirituality Without Religion* is the written vehicle, or "bible," through which he seeks to accomplish his "mission."

The common non-religious man who is ignorant of esoteric spirituality will likely be impressed with Harris's discourse in *Waking Up*. But the cognoscenti, experts in the Awakening project and the Great Spiritual Traditions (including, but not limited to, Pali, Zen, and Tibetan Buddhism, Advaita Vedanta, Kashmir Shaivism, Kabbalah, Daism, and Christian Hermeticism) will not be. They will see Harris for what he is: a pretender outside his element who reduces "waking up" to his own level of understanding.

My guess is that Harris saw how successful *Buddha's Brain* by (fellow deluded neuroscientist) Rick Hanson was (see my review), and decided to pen his own text on "waking up" within an essentially Buddhist context. Money talks, and even though Buddhist bullshit walks, it brings in mucho moolah for big-name scientists who peddle it, such as Harris.

Pompous Pontifications of an Un-Initiated Mystic

In *Waking Up*, Harris criticizes Aldous Huxley's and others' vision of the Perennial Philosophy, arguing that it is essentially chimera because the Abrahamic religions are "incorrigibly dualistic," and thus cannot be equated with nondualistic Buddhism and Hindu Advaita Vedanta. I not only contend that Harris is wrong, but in my writings I present an esoteric trinitarian version of the Perennial Philosophy that exceeds Huxley's (see my review of *The Perennial Philosophy*), Frithjof Schuon's (see my review of *The Transcendent Unity of Religions*), and Rudolf Otto's (see my review of *The Idea of the Holy*). If

Harris could look a little deeper, he'd realize that the putatively nondual Eastern traditions are only nominally nondual.
In fact, unbeknownst to Harris, a remedial student of Tibetan
Dzogchen, the Buddhist *Trikaya* (*Dharmakaya*, *Sambhogakaya*,
Nirmanakaya) mirrors the Christian Trinity, and the practice
of Dzogchen is essentially the same as the mystical, or esoteric, Eucharist.

In *Waking Up*, Harris is guilty of the common reductionism
and Dharma distortion that plague modern Buddhism. For example, he writes: "The deepest goal of spirituality is freedom
from the illusion of the self." No, it's not; it's achieving *Nirvana*,
or *Bodhicitta*, which is tantamount to Hindu Self-realization.
The Buddha did not teach that there is no self; he taught that
no Self could be found in the five *skandhas* (grasping groups).
Any bloke can observe that his bodymind is in constant flux
and thus does not constitute a changeless self or entity. But
such a realization is rudimentary, far from the "deepest goal
of spirituality," which, unbeknownst to Harris, is union with
the Spirit (or *Sambhogakaya*, or Stream), the Clear-Light Energy that "produces," or unveils, permanent En-Light-enment,
Nirvana.

But because Harris is an "un-initiated," or "un-baptized,"
spiritual practitioner, he has no experience or understanding of consciousness as Spirit, or *Shakti*—meaning the dynamic force-flow (termed *Kundalini*, which moves through
the "coils," or *nadis*, of one's etheric body), and no compre-
hension of how this *Shakti*, or Light-Energy, divinizes, or en-

Light-ens, a yogi, enabling him to Awaken. If Harris had an esoteric bone in his body and had been "initiated" (what the Buddha termed becoming a "Stream-winner"), he'd realize that the Buddha was called the "Blessed One" because he was Blessed/Blissed by Light-Energy (the Stream, or *Sambhoga-kaya*, or *Dharmamegha*), the Supernal Inflow that precipitates the Nirvanic "drying up of the outflows" and (what the Buddha called) the "Heart [or Consciousness]-release" (which I'll elaborate shortly, when I discuss Ramana Maharshi and Harris's failure to grok him).

Harris deserves credit for at least being a serious spiritual seeker—but, unfortunately, he is not a finder. He describes his journey to the East and his encounters with his two "gurus" after he attempted to move beyond Burmese master U Pandita Sayadaw's Vipassana meditation instructions. His first guru was H.W.L. Poonja (1910-1997), commonly known as Papaji (see my review of his book *Truth Is*). Because Harris lacks spiritual discrimination, he mistakenly considered Papaji to have been as Enlightened as his guru, Sri Ramana Maharshi (1879-1950), who, unlike Papaji, "cracked the spiritual code" (see my reviews of *Talks with Sri Ramana Maharshi*, *Sri Ramana Gita*, and *Sat Darshana Bhashya*).

If Harris had read and grokked Ramana Maharshi, he'd be a step ahead of his fellow brain scientists, because he'd realize that the root locus of the mind—where consciousness intersects a human being before it "crystallizes" as thought-forms, or mind, in the brain—is the spiritual Heart-center (*Hridayam* in Hinduism, *Tathagatagarbha* in Buddhism), located two digits to the right of the center of one's chest. The human soul-matrix, one's complex of psychical seed tendencies, or "storehouse consciousness" (*Alaya-vijnana* in Yogacara), is located here in the incarnated human vehicle. But Harris has nothing to say about the Heart-center and its relation to the mind and the brain.

If Harris understood the En-Light-enment project, he would also know that it is only through the descent of the *Shakti*, or *Sambhogakaya* (which is literally sucked into the *Hridayam*, along with the mind, the "crystallized" outflow of psychical seed tendencies), that one can Awaken. It is the *Shakti*, or Stream, that precipitates the "Heart-release," which grants Nirvana. Nirvana, or Self-realization, is achieved when the Heart-knot is cut (which Ramana Maharshi describes in detail in his esoteric teachings). When the Heart-knot is cut, universal (timeless, spaceless) Consciousness radiates ceaselessly through the now-open "Heart-hole." This Consciousness, or Awareness, is the One Mind, described by great Zen masters, such as Huang Po. But Harris, a pompous and deluded pontificator, assures us that there is no such thing as the One Mind.

Harris talks about realizing that the self/individual "I" is an illusion, but he never mentions that when this "illusion" is transcended, one awakens to the true, or transcendental, "I," the true Self, or Buddha-nature, which both Hindu and Buddhist masters describe. (For example, the iconic Dzogchen master Longchen Rabjam, in his *A Treasure Trove of Scriptural Transmis-*

sion, writes: "'I' means the heart essence... 'I' refers to the awakened mind.") But Harris, in line with most contemporary Buddhist teachers/writers, never moves beyond denying the reality of the self to asserting the Reality of the Self, the true "I," or Buddha-nature.

After Papaji failed to Enlighten Harris, he moved on from Advaita Vedanta to Dzogchen. Unfortunately, his choice of gurus was no better. He became a student of Tulku Urgyen Rinpoche (1920-1996), an overrated Dzogchen master (see my reviews of his *Rainbow Painting* and *Quintessential Dzogchen*).

Harris, briefly, attempts to describe Dzogchen meditation (which consists of the two complementary practices of *trekcho* and *togal*), but he does a poor job explaining *trekcho* (cutting through spiritual materialism to get to Spirit, the *Sambhogakaya*), and he doesn't even mention *togal* (conducting the Spirit-current, or Clear-Light continuum), because, as an un-initiated (by the Spirit) mystic, he has no experience or understanding of it.

The Skinny on Sam

Sam Harris is a Jew, an Aries (Sun sign), and a scientific materialist. Jews (and I am one) are usually outspoken with their opinions. Combine Jewishness with Aries (the most self-assertive sign in the zodiac) and you get a veritable big-mouth pontificator. A classic example of this combination is the late, renowned sports announcer Howard Cosell, who turned the broadcasting booth into his personal pulpit. Add scientific materialism to the Jewish-Aries mix, and you get an individual intent on spreading the gospel of atheism while demeaning religion. In short, you get "Soapbox" Sam.

Harris has opinions on almost everything, and he's never shy about expressing them, even though most of them are laughed at by the cognoscenti, who turn their noses up at the drivel disseminated by the Matrix-bound Sam. For example, Harris's political opinions are typically statist "solutions" which "those in the know" (meaning Objectivists, libertarians, and trans-zeitgeistians) reject as liberal-fascist. The fact that Harris was delusional enough to support "Crooked" Hillary over Donald Trump in the 2016 U.S. presidential election, and then "Beijing" Biden over Trump in 2020, exemplifies his political ignorance.

One of the foremost contemporary sociopolitical commentators is Stefan Molyneux (check out his website: freedomain. com). But Harris, doubtless knowing that he would get his clock cleaned, refuses at this time to debate Molyneux. Harris's excuse for avoiding Molyneux is that he has enabled racists by interviewing racialists who emphasize IQ and other distinctions among races. This, of course, is a cop-out, because Molyneux, in his quest for the truth (and unlike the zeitgeist-bound Harris), is not circumscribed regarding the subjects he will broach. Moreover, Molyneux, a secular philosopher par excellence, would decimate the philosophically challenged Harris on his pet topics, including free will and morality.

It doesn't, however, take a Molyneux-level brainiac to deconstruct Harris's philosophic hokum. A read of the book *The Sam
Harris Delusion* by Mike Hockney (available at Amazon Kindle)
will convince most everyone of Harris's philosophic deficien-
cies, and arm them with a plethora of arguments that make a
monkey of him.

Harris clearly uses just one side (or half) of his brain. If he
had developed feeling-intuition, he wouldn't mock astrology
as he does (even putting down the Dalai Lama for consulting
an astrologer); rather, he would realize that people, in general,
fit their Sun signs. I'm a former professional astrologer, and I
laugh at those such as Harris who put down astrology without
having studied it. The great Isaac Newton, when asked by a
fellow scientist how he could believe in astrology, replied, "I
have studied it, you haven't."

Harris, one of the God-dissing "Four Horsemen" (Richard
Dawkins, Christopher Hitchens, and Daniel Dennett are the
other three), is renowned for his championing of atheism. Yet,
neither of the spiritual traditions of Harris's two gurus (Advaita Vedanta/Papaji, Dzogchen/Tulku Urgyen Rinpoche) are
atheistic. But the acausal God, or Being, of these traditions,
which is timeless Consciousness, or Awareness, itself, is apparently beyond the apprehension of the spiritually challenged
Harris. In fact, the *Kunjed Gyalpo* (tr. "The All-Creating Mon-
arch"), the fundamental Tantra of the Dzogchen Semde (one
of the three Series that comprise Dzogchen teachings), is all
about a Supreme Source, or Divine Being—Samantabhadra—

who is also a Creator God; but Harris, conveniently, never broaches this subject.

I could continue deconstructing Harris, but since this is just an article and not a book (which I plan to eventually pen on Harris), I'll close here by summarizing my view on his text *Waking up: A Guide to Spirituality Without Religion*: The title is a gross misnomer, because there isn't a shred of spirituality in the text. Harris has nothing to say about the Spirit (*Sambhoga-kaya*, or Stream, in Buddhism), because he hasn't experienced it and is clueless regarding its role in Awakening. While those new to Eastern philosophy might benefit from his book, why bother when far better texts on Awakening are available? As for spiritual veterans, they will find Harris's book good for one thing: fuel for the fireplace.

CHAPTER SEVEN

Dark Buddhism

*D*ark Buddhism: Integrating Zen Buddhism and Objectivism is a book by Morgan D. Rosenberg that seeks to reconcile Zen Buddhism with Ayn Rand's Objectivism. While I respect Rosenberg's effort, I have little regard for his "Dark Buddhism," because his grasp of Buddhadharma does not exceed a pop Zen level, and he fails to creatively and esoterically integrate Zen and Objectivism. Below is my review of Rosenberg's book (which was originally posted at Amazon, and then deleted by Amazon along with the rest of my 300-plus book reviews). My review summarizes my criticism of his Dark Buddhism, but rather than just criticize his book, I decided to also describe my vision of Dark Buddhism, the description of which follows my review.

My Review of *Dark Buddhism*

The author of this book, physicist Morgan D. Rosenberg, typifies the numerous professors and scientists who are attracted to Buddhism and think that their worldly success and intelligence somehow qualify them to write books on the subject. But as an authority on Buddhism (and Objectivism), I laugh at their efforts. In fact, though I read and review one Buddhism book after another, I have yet to encounter a living professor or scientist who truly groks Buddhism.

In this text, Rosenberg attempts to marry Buddhism with Ayn Rand's Objectivism, and he audaciously terms his concoction "Dark Buddhism." But the marriage is a failure because Rosenberg's understanding of Buddhism (both original and Zen) doesn't exceed a basic level. Most tellingly, he recommends Steve Hagen's retarded text *Buddhism Plain and Simple* (see my review), and the Buddhadharma he espouses reflects Hagen's.

Although I'm a huge fan of Rand's Objectivism (see my review of her *Introduction to Objectivist Epistemology*), as is Rosenberg, the problem with Objectivists is that they are allergic to mysticism, and thus incapable of differentiating mystical hokum from esoteric spirituality, the reality of which they reject. Although some Objectivists, such as Rosenberg, gravitate to Buddhism because they perceive it as atheistic, scientific, and non-mystical, in truth, it is none of these. Rather, it is ultra-mystical, pointing its adherents to an ineffable Reality that the Buddha termed *Nirvana*. But Rosenberg, a smug, flat intellectual, reduces Buddhism to his own shrunken level of understanding, and the result, in this book, is a perversion of genuine Buddhadharma.

Rosenberg's reduction, or de-esotericization, of Buddhism is exemplified by his fallacious description of the eighth and culminating limb of Buddha's Noble Eightfold Path. He writes: "The final aspect of the Eightfold Path is right meditation or right concentration. Right meditation is freeing the mind from distraction so that your thoughts become focused, centered, and aware." This is a gross misrepresentation of this limb, which is Right Contemplation, which is all about the Four *Jhanas* (or *Samadhis*), which are states of infused contemplation involving degrees of absorption in the Stream, or Spirit-current. There can be no attainment of Nirvana without the *jhanas*, but Rosenberg not only doesn't understand this, he doesn't understand Nirvana, which he mistakenly conflates with *satori*. Moreover, the cognoscenti can only laugh at those such as Rosenberg and Hagen, who, pathetically, reduce Enlightenment to "seeing things as they are."

Rosenberg's descriptions of meditation reflect his own limited experience and development. And the fact that his own practice employs a mantra and visualization reveals the beginner's level he is at. I have no problem with spiritual neophytes, but when they assume the role of a pontificating teacher, as Rosenberg does, it raises my hackles.

I could spend pages deconstructing Rosenberg's faulty, dumbed-down Buddhadharma, but I have better things to do with my time. Instead, I'll end my review by briefly commenting on his central thesis: the distinction between his Dark Buddhism and traditional Buddhism. Rosenberg writes, "Philosophically the most glaring difference between Dark Buddhism and traditional Buddhism is that the Buddha taught dissolution of the self, whereas Dark Buddhism reintegrates the self into the philosophy and, particularly, directs itself to fostering healthy and strong self-esteem."

The Buddha did not teach dissolution of the self. He taught that no Self could be found in the Five *Skandhas* (or Aggregates). The Buddha would laugh at anyone "smuggling" self-esteem into his Dharma and renaming it Dark Buddhism. Self-esteem has nothing whatsoever to do with Buddhism, which is all about awakening to a supramundane Reality that frees one from, among other things, concern about one's self-status.

I'd ordinarily give a butchered Buddhism book like this a lone star, but the fact that Rosenberg champions Objectivism, while correctly pointing out some of its flaws, merits an additional star.

My "Dark Buddhism"

Although it's difficult to integrate Buddhism with Objectivism because of the myriad contradictions between the two teachings, Objectivism has aspects that can serve to improve Buddhadharma. But before I consider them, I first want to delve into another "dark" (or perhaps I should say "taboo") side of Buddhism: its similarities with Hinduism and Christianity. As I've learned from my exchanges with Buddhists at Facebook and Amazon, these people are often loath to consider these similarities. They maintain a condescending attitude toward other religions, and unlike the Hindus, who generally embrace the Perennial Philosophy (which perceives the essence of the major religions to be the same), they make it a point to emphasize distinctions, rather than commonalities, between Buddhism and other religions.

The late Chinese Buddhist scholar Professor Garma C.C. Chang (1920-1988) exemplifies the smug, learned Buddhist who takes potshots at Hinduism, identifying it as inferior to Buddhism. In his book *The Buddhist Teaching of Totality: The Philosophy of Hwa Yen Buddhism*, Dr. Chang writes: "Now the Buddhist stand on the intuitive feeling of Being or thatness is diametrically opposed to that of the Upanishads and Aquinas. Instead of glorifying the 'beingness' and augmenting its significance to theological or soteriological levels, Buddhists believe that this intuitive grasping of being, or actuality, is an expression of men's deep clinging and attachment. It is the very root of all sufferings and delusions in samsara!"

Unfortunately, Dr. Chang doesn't know what he's talking about. First off, there is no clinging in Being, because Being, by definition, is the end of becoming (*samsara*), of grasping after successive (contracted) states of being. In other words, Buddhist Nirvana is the same "State" (or non-state) as Hindu Being. Moreover, the "feeling of Being" that Dr. Chang denigrates is the spontaneous Bliss (or *Ananda*) that all Enlightened sages (in all religions) experience, and it involves no grasping whatsoever. It is, in fact, the very same Bliss that a Buddha spontaneously enjoys via the *Sambhogakaya* (the Blessing/Blissing Clear-Light Energy Body).

Culadasa (John Yates, PhD), author of the uber-popular *The Mind Illuminated: A Complete Meditation Guide Integrating Buddhist Wisdom and Brain Science for Greater Mindfulness* (see my review), is a contemporary Buddhist teacher revered by many for his

Dharma wisdom. But I'm not one of the many, because I find his Dharma problematic.

One of my problems with Culadasa is his teaching of no-Self. The Buddha himself did not explicitly state whether there is a transcendental Self. But his teaching of *Anatta* implies that there is, for it rejects the five aggregates as not-Self, which leaves the Self, or Buddha-nature (which is pure Awareness, or Consciousness), as one's True Nature, or Identity. In other words, a Buddha is one who is Awareness itself. If he were not this Awareness, he could not remain permanently, unbrokenly Awake, or Aware.

According to Culadasa, when one asks, "Who is conscious?" the answer is the "collective of minds that constitute the mind-system." This is the wrong answer, because the spiritual illuminati (including innumerable great Buddhist masters) know that it is Consciousness, or Mind, itself that is conscious of all phenomena it encounters, not a bunch of mini-minds in one's head. Culadasa's collectivist mind-system represents a perverted, exoteric interpretation of the Yogacara school of Buddhism, wherefrom he derives it. The highest Yogacara teaching, exemplified in the *Lankavatara Sutra*, emphasizes that the unborn, transcendental Self-Mind is the Reality behind and beyond all cognized objects.

Culadasa's point of view regarding the transcendental Self is in diametrical opposition to India's greatest twentieth-century spiritual master, the iconic Ramana Maharshi. According to Maharshi, when a yogi, via the practice of Self-enquiry, seeks the

answer to who or what watches and experiences, the Answer is
the Self, which is Consciousness itself. But Culadasa, clearly not
a Self-realized master, writes:

> Mistaking the witness state for a True Self is what leads
> some people to claim that Consciousness is the True Self.
> To properly use the Witness experience, probe more deep-
> ly. Go to the Still Point, the place of the Witness, with a
> question: "Who or what is this Witness?" Who is watching?
> Who is experiencing? Adamantly refuse to entertain any
> answers offered by your intellectual, thinking mind. Also,
> don't be deceived by your emotional mind, which will try
> to make you believe you've the answer when you haven't.
> Just hold on to the question as you experience the Witness.
> If and when Insight arises, it will be a profound Insight into
> the truth of no-Self, and it will be so obvious you'll wonder
> why you never realized it before.

This paragraph by Culadasa displays his ignorance. Innumerable yogis have realized the Self by seeking the Who that experiences and watches. But the ordinary person, who lacks the
ability to draw down *Shakti* (the *Sambhogakaya*, or Stream) into
the Spiritual Heart-center (the *Hridayam*, or *Tathagatagarbha*),
located (or felt-experienced) two digits to the right of the center of one's chest), cannot have a true Self experience. This is
the case because the Self is *Siva-Shakti* (or *Dharmakaya-Sam-
bhogakaya*). So until the *Shakti*, at least temporarily, converges with one's individual consciousness (immanent *siva*), in
the Spiritual Heart-center, the luminous Self (a.k.a. Mind, or
Buddha) cannot be experienced.

Dark Buddhism, to my mind, means, among other things, identifying Mind (or Buddha, or Self), and not emptiness (a non-existent with no ontological status), as Ultimate Reality. And because the vast majority of modern Buddhist writers are afflicted with what I call the "Madhyamaka virus," (meaning the identification of Ultimate Reality as emptiness rather than as Mind), as I see it, anyone who champions Mind as Reality is, knowingly or unknowingly, promoting Dark Buddhism.

Culadasa and Garma C.C. Chang are just two examples of the innumerable modern Buddhist writers who emphasize the no-Self/Self distinction between Buddhism and Hinduism. But my Dark Buddhism sees this distinction as false, because, as the spiritual cognoscenti know, Mind = Buddha = Self—and Mind, not emptiness, is the *Dharmakaya*, the Truth (or Reality) Dimension (or Body) that equates to Hindu *Siva*, which is universal Consciousness (or Mind, or Being).

Even more "dark" than equating Hinduism with Buddhism is equating Christianity with it. But to the cognoscenti, there are so many parallels between the two religions that not viewing them as kissing cousins is tantamount to spiritual myopia. Just as Gautama the Buddha, the Blessed One, was Blessed by the Stream, likewise Jesus the Christ was Blessed by the Holy Spirit, the same Body, or Hypostasis, as the Stream—later renamed the *Sambhogakaya* in Mahayana Buddhism. And just as Buddha pointed his disciples to Nirvana, Jesus pointed his to Heaven, the same eternal, or timeless, Reality.

The parallels between Buddhism and Christianity become even more compelling when one considers later Trinitarian Christianity in the context of Mahayana/Vajrayana Buddhism. This is primarily so because the Buddhist *Trikaya*, which first emerged in Mahayana, is, when properly explicated, a near-perfect match for the esoteric Christian Trinity. Moreover, although Buddhism denies the existence of a soul, the Eighth Consciousness in Yogacara, the *Alaya-Vijnana*, can be construed as a match for the human soul. Renowned spiritual author Deepak Chopra explains:

> The Eighth Consciousness is a term what some people call soul. Although Buddhism always says that there is no soul, what it means is that there is no absolute soul. So what Buddhism refers to as the Eighth Consciousness is what many non-Buddhists would say is their soul. In particular, this Eighth Consciousness survives the death of the body, and along with its life energy departs for some other place. When it sees the new father and mother, it mixes with their sperm and ovum and becomes a new person.

Objectivism and Buddhism

Although contradictions abound between Objectivism and Buddhism, there is still much in Rand's philosophy that can benefit Buddhists. First, Rand's view on emptiness, which contradicts Nagarjuna's, should give Mahayana Buddhists pause for thought. Per Rand, emptiness is a non-existent with no ontological status; hence it is simply a derivative term that implies the absence of something. Just as the Buddha rejected emptiness as Ultimate Reality, so does Objectivism. Therefore, my Dark Buddhism, in accordance with Objectivism, rejects Madhyamaka's emptiness doctrine.

Whereas Madhyamaka posits emptiness as the most fundamental axiom, Objectivism identifies existence and consciousness as axiomatic. In Rand's novel *Atlas Shrugged*, the hero, John Galt, explains:

> Whatever the degree of your knowledge, these two—existence and consciousness—are axioms you cannot escape, these two are the irreducible primaries implied in any action you undertake, in any part of your knowledge and in its sum, from the first ray of light you perceive at the start of your life to the widest erudition you might acquire at its end. Whether you know the shape of a pebble or the structure of a solar system, the axioms remain the same: that *it* exists and that you *know* it.
>
> To exist is to be something, as distinguished from the nothing of non-existence, it is to be an entity of a specific nature made of specific attributes. Centuries ago, the man who was—no matter what his errors—the greatest of your philosophers, has stated the formula defining the concept of existence and the rule of all knowledge: *A is A*. A thing is itself. You have never grasped the meaning of his statement. I am here to complete it: Existence is Identity, Consciousness is Identification.

To exist is to exist as "something." If one extends this axiom to the universal Existent, or Being, its Identity, per spiritual masters, is identified as Mind, the transcendental and immanent Buddha. This raises the question: Is Mind a thing? Yes, but not a created or space-time thing. Rather, it is the Self-Existing, Self-Radiant Being (or Consciousness)—sometimes referred to as the "Thing-in-Itself"—wherefrom all manifest existents stem. And though this "Thing," or Being, is shapeless and formless, as well as timeless and spaceless, it is not emptiness, which, again, is a non-existent with no ontological status.

When Rand defines consciousness as identification, she delimits the term to mean the identification of manifest existents. But consciousness is also able to identify itself as the unmanifest Existent, or Being, which is possible because its Nature is biunial, consisting not only of Awareness, but also Clear-Light Energy, which, through the medium of an En-Light-ened mystic, reflects Awareness (or Consciousness) back to Itself as radiant Being-Consciousness (the *Dharmakaya*).

Is it possible to explain the en-Light-enment process via Objectivist principles? Absolutely. The spiritual practice that en-Light-ens a disciple is simply an amped-up version of Objectivism, so to speak. It is the conscious process of maintaining full ontological context, which awakens and intensifies the radiant Spirit-current, which en-Light-ens one.

Rand says that consciousness, via the process of mental abstraction, is the faculty that identifies reality. Moreover, she says that logic—non-contradictory identification of reality—is the method for identifying reality. Rand is correct, but only on an epistemic level. If a disciple establishes and maintains a yogic (meaning a direct, immediate ontic) connection of conscious at-one-ment with reality prior to retracting into mental abstraction, then the consciousness-force engendered by this connection translates into Spirit-power.

Rand says that "spirit" means "pertaining to consciousness." While this is also correct, she has no understanding of the relationship between Spirit-power and consciousness-force on an ontic, or yogic, level.

Rand understood the principle of logic, which is mental, but not the principle of what I call onto-logic, which is spiritual, and which antecedes and supersedes cognition. Onto-logic is simply another term for yoga. Yoga is about directly connecting to, and communing with, Reality, prior to retracting into mental abstraction, which contracts one's field of consciousness and flow of Spirit-energy.

You Really Need to Enter the Stream

The epitome of my Dark Buddhism pertains to Stream-entry. I contend that En-Light-enment can only be attained by entering the Stream, a.k.a. the *Sambhogakaya*, the Light-Energy continuum of the *Dharmakaya*. The Four *Jhanas*, which constitute Right Contemplation, the final limb of Buddha's Noble Eightfold Path, describe progressively fuller immersions in the Stream, and culminate in *Bodhicitta*, or Nirvana.

I'm not the only Buddhist that emphasizes the importance of Stream-entry in the En-Light-enment project. The Zennist blog (zennist.typepad.com) also advances this same mystical, or "Dark Zen," point of view. Below is an article ("You Really Need to Enter the Stream") from the blog, which makes clear the need for Buddhas-in-the-making to be baptized in the Stream, or Spirit-current:

> It almost goes without saying, but Western Buddhists are not, by and large, students of the Sutras (P., Suttas), hence all the freaking arguments that tend to erupt. I suspect that most pop Buddhist writers haven't studied but a handful of Sutras. It is when debates arise over certain key doctrines such as Atman vs. no-self that Sutras become important. But they are also important for understanding meditation and the Five Aggregates (pañca-skandha) and their relationship to our self and why we are not these conditioned aggregates.
>
> The problem facing the novice is what do the specific terms mean as to their notion. What is the specific notion of anât-man (lit., not the self) or pratityasamutpada (dependent origination), or dhyâna (meditation), or vijñâna (consciousness)? What does nirvana mean? Incidentally, even the best scholars have to make educated guesses when it comes to nirvana—not all agree with each other. We see this in the book, The Buddhist Nirvana and Its Western Interpreters by Guy Richard Welbon.
>
> Speaking from the vantage point of the Pali Nikayas, it is only when we have entered the stream or current (S.,

srotas), a kind of super spiritual baptism, that we begin to understand the Buddha's terms as they are meant to be understood.

"Better than absolute sovereignty on the earth, better than going to heaven, better than lordship over all the worlds is the reward (phalam) of entering the stream (sotapatti)" (Dhammapada 178).

During this baptism, we get our first glimpse of nirvana. In addition, we begin to distinguish our psychophysical body from our true self. We also put away our doubts about the veracity of the Buddha's teachings because we now can see what he is aiming at. As a result, we no longer cling to ritualistic and moralistic practices which really amount to dead-ends. Short of this, our understanding of Buddhism is like that of a man born blind before he is cured by a physician. He insists that his senses are correct (this was an argument the Buddha used against materialists).

Summary

Dark Buddhism, as I conceive it, is characterized by five factors: 1) It embraces "the Esoteric Perennial Philosophy," which considers the esoteric (or truly spiritual) essence of the three major religions (Christianity, Hinduism, and Buddhism) to be the same; 2) it rejects Madhyamaka's illogical and non-spiritual *sunyata* teaching; 3) it denies that true Buddhism teaches a no-Self doctrine; 4) it integrates pertinent aspects of Ayn Rand's Objectivism; and 5) it emphasizes the role of the Stream, or *Sambhogakaya*, in the En-Light-enment project.

My Dark Buddhism is "dark" only because mainstream Buddhism rejects the five factors it embraces. When it no longer rejects them, then my Dark Buddhism will cease to exist, for its "darkness" will have been eclipsed by its light.

CHAPTER EIGHT

Zen Mind, Non-Thinker's Mind

Seng Ts'an, the third Zen patriarch, famously declared: "Stop talking, stop thinking, and there is nothing you will not understand." Was he right? Hardly. And if one examines the history of Zen, this becomes blatantly evident. The following subchapters, excerpted from my book *Beyond the Power of Now*, provide evidence that contradicts Seng Ts'an's statement.

Zen and Creativity

In the book *Wild Ivy*, the Zen master Hakuin (1686–1768) and other Zen monks develop energy disorders as a result of their meditation practice. But all their years of mind-emptying meditation fails to provide them with a *satori*-inspired solution to their problem, and the Zen tradition itself has no answer for their disease. In order to cure themselves, the Zen master and the monks are forced to resort to the Taoist tradition, which, unlike the Zen tradition, emphasizes a holistic rather than a quasi-nihilistic approach toward life. If Zen were a creative tradition, like Taoism and Hinduism, it would have developed "in-house" remedies for problems such as Hakuin's.

If great scientific discoveries are mainly dependent on "no-mind" rather than mind, then why have most been made by men with stratospheric IQs and extensive education? Creative breakthroughs do often come at times of mental quietude. But this isn't because the mind has stopped working; it's because the subconscious mind has been working on the problem all along, and when the conscious mind temporarily relaxes its efforts, the answers spring forth from the subconscious. To those unfamiliar with modern psychology—including Einstein and the hundred leading physicists who, in 1900, participated in mathematician Jacques Hadamard's survey (see *Psychology of Invention in the Mathematical Field* by Jacques Hadamard)—it might indeed seem that great insights arise from a mystical "place" beyond conscious thought. But that "place" isn't the "realm of no-mind"; it's the "realm of the individual's subconscious mind," which confers creative insights only in response to the individual's *previous* conscious efforts.

The mind is not consciousness itself. Consciousness, the essence of Being, is a universal constant that exists prior to and beyond thought. The mind is a function or application of consciousness that enables you to mentally understand the universe you live in. When you think, you are using the uniquely human faculty of mind, which, via the process of concept formation, is able to create mental "concretes" which accurately measure and reflect the world you perceive through your senses. Thinking enables you to measure (or *ratio*-nally compare, contrast, and comprehend) the sensible universe—that which

has been "measured out" as a manifestation of the Unmanifest-
ed—and, via concepts, form intelligent and creative conclu-
sions about the things you perceive. Thinking, in other words,
is a nonpareil tool for measuring conditional reality, the manifested. And when thinking is rejected, you end up with a Zen
tradition that, unlike Taoism and Hinduism, has no solution for
meditation-induced energy disorders.

Eckhart Tolle, the uber-popular guru, loves to use Zen stories
to make a spiritual point, because like most Zen masters, he
has little regard for the human mind, particularly its ability
to intelligently discriminate or measure reality. Unsurpris-
ingly, he also claims that "the human mind is not creative."
Tolle uses the story of Zen master Banzan becoming enlightened in a butcher shop to illustrate the point that spiritual
awakening can stem from merely accepting every "cut of meat"
(or "every moment of life") as "the best." In other words, if you
can somehow convince yourself that everything that exists in a
present moment—including rape, murder, genocide, and pol-
lution—is truly hunky-dory, truly for the best, then you too
can become an enlightened Zen master.

Zen at War

The following excerpt from Josh Baran's book review of *Zen
at War* by Brian Victoria, available at baranstrategies.com/
blog/2016/4/zen-holy-war, provides an eye-opening look at
the Japanese Zen establishment's complicity with Japan's im-
perial war machine in the nineteenth and twentieth centuries.

It demonstrates what can happen when the right thinking prescribed by Gautama Buddha is rejected in favor of mindless non-thinking:

> Zen at War is a courageous and exhaustively researched book by Brian Victoria, a western Soto Zen priest and instructor at the University of Auckland. Victoria reveals the inside story of the Japanese Zen establishment's dedicated support of the imperial war machine from the late 1880's through World War 2. He chronicles in detail how prominent Zen leaders perverted the Buddhist teaching to encourage blind obedience, mindless killing, and total devotion to the emperor. The consequences were catastrophic and the impact can still be felt today.

> Victoria identifies Sawaki Kodo (1880–1965), one of the great Soto Zen patriarchs of this [20th] century, as an evangelical war proponent. Serving in Russia as a soldier, he happily related how he and his comrades had "gorged ourselves on killing people." Later, in 1942, he wrote, "It is just to punish those who disturb the public order. Whether one kills or does not kill, the precept forbidding killing [is preserved]. It is the precept that wields the sword. It is the precept that throws the bomb."

> The "precept throws the bomb?" This is an astonishing abuse of Zen language. Kodo also advocated, as did other Zen teachers, that if killing is done without thinking, in a state of no-mind or no-self, then the act is an expression of enlightenment. No thinking = No-mind = No-self =

No karma. In this bizarre equation, the victims are always left out, as if they were irrelevant. Killing is just an elegant expression of the *koan*.

When Colonel Aizawa Saburo was being tried for murdering another general in 1935, he testified, "I was in an absolute sphere, so there was neither affirmation nor negation, neither good nor evil." This approach to Zen is ultimately a perverse narcissism, or even nihilism. Of course, the obvious question that was never asked—if there is no self, why is there any need to kill?

Victoria has brought to light the actual words of those leaders and the written record of this period. *Zen at War* contains dozens of similar passages from leading teachers, proving that this distortion was the rule, not the exception. There were some pacifists, but they were few. Some priests who opposed the war may have quietly retired to distant country temples, but they probably left no record.

The marriage of Zen and the Japanese war machine demonstrates how warped a mind-averse ideology can become in the heat of a hellish political climate. Because Zen is a tunnel-vision religion that focuses on the now while disparaging the mind that dwells on the past and the future, it never developed the strong ethical foundation that characterizes most other schools of Buddhism. Hence, while ideals such as compassion and non-violence are emphasized in non-Zen Buddhist sects, in Zen they are dismissed as superfluous concepts to be expunged from one's mind. The popular Zen saying, "If you meet the Buddha on the road, kill him," perfectly summarizes the Japanese Zen attitude toward anything mind-based, including the moral ideals so essential to making the world a more peaceful place.

The Flag and Objective Reality

The following fabled, didactic Zen exchange illustrates just how oblivious to reality some Zen mystics can be:

> Zen Student #1 (observing a flag waving in the wind): The flag is moving.
>
> Zen Student #2: No, the wind is moving.
>
> Zen Student #3: No, you're both wrong. The mind is moving.

What this Zen exchange illustrates is nothing less than an utter indictment of man's conceptual faculty. From the Zen perspective, the moral of this story is that Zen Student #3 is correct, that your mind is incapable of accurately perceiving and interpreting objective reality. You see a flag waving in the wind, but it's just an illusion! If your mind is perfectly still, then there is no movement, and hence no time. This type of nonsensical mysticism stems from the wish to assert the primacy of consciousness over existence. In other words, reality is made to conform to your mind (or no-mind) instead of your mind, *properly*, being made to conform to reality.

CHAPTER NINE

Buddhist Politics 501

According to the Pew Research Center's party affiliation among Buddhists by political ideology survey in 2014 (http://www.pewforum.org/religious-landscape-study/compare/political-ideology/by/party-affiliation/among/religious-tradition/buddhist/), 12% of American Buddhists identify themselves as conservatives, 32% as moderates, 54% as liberals, and 2% "don't know." There is little reason to doubt the veracity of this survey because other such surveys provide similar results.

Left-wing Buddhists not only outnumber right-wingers by more than a 4/1 ratio, but many of them are now devoted to combining Buddhism with a "progressive" political agenda. At his blog Hardcore Zen (hardcorezen.info), Brad Warner comments on this phenomenon:

> What bugs me is when it appears that liberal, left-leaning Buddhists are trying to mix Buddhism with their political agenda in precisely the same way people like Pat Robertson mix Christianity with their conservative political agenda. This just makes us all look bad to everyone except lefty types who already agree with whatever cause is being espoused. Nobody is going to be convinced to

change their views on militarism or global warming because they saw a photo of a bunch of weirdos in costumes they associate with cult members holding a banner outside of the White House. It is an exercise in vanity, which can only serve to help entrench people's previously established views.

In contrast to Brad Warner, I have no problem with Buddhists pushing a political agenda, I just have a problem with their "liberal" agenda, which is contrary to what the Buddha taught. This liberal agenda is based on the forceful (socialistic) transference of wealth, which amounts to theft, a violation of a fundamental Buddhist tenet. At her blog ThoughtCo. (thoughtco. com), Barbara O'Brien comments on this:

> The second Buddhist precept often is translated "do not steal." Some Buddhist teachers prefer "practice generosity." A more literal translation of the early Pali texts is "I undertake the precept to refrain from taking that which is not given."

Because this theft of money entails force and violence—the government will imprison you if you don't pay what they demand—the left-wing agenda of wealth transference not only violates the second Buddhist precept, but also the first: non-killing, which extends to include non-violence. As the website Clear Vision (www. clear-vision.org) puts it:

> Buddhists have always interpreted this [the first] precept to mean, not merely a prohibition of murder, but of all kinds of violence against human beings and animals.

What left-wingers fail to grasp is the difference between voluntary communal activity and coercive statist socialism. While the former is non-violent, the latter isn't. The State typically devolves into an authoritarian, Leviathan monster that fascistically and Orwellianly dictates how people live their lives and spend their money. It becomes a monolithic corruptocracy, wherein politicians, who are bought off by big-money special interests, enact legislation that delimits the (putatively guaranteed) constitutional rights of the country's citizens, who, brainwashed by public schools, left-wing universities, and the mainstream media, willingly obey, and even worship, their Big Government masters.

Because American Buddhists are big on compassion, on helping the poor and needy, they typically support government aid programs such as welfare, food stamps, and housing subsidies. But these programs, over the decades, have proved to be an abysmal failure, and rather than helping the downtrodden, they have, in effect, enslaved them, making them dependent and dysfunctional. For example, in 1960, 80% of black children were born into two-parent families, but now, a half century after the War on Poverty was begun under President Lyndon Johnson, that figure is down to 30%. In other words, the welfare state, initiated by Johnson in 1964, has decimated the black nuclear family. It has done so by incentivizing black women to have lots of kids sans a husband, because the more such children a woman has, the larger her welfare check will be. The black man, meanwhile, divorced from a supportive family structure, often turns to crime and ends up in prison. But mindless left-wingers continue to want to waste billions of taxpayers' dollars on social programs that not only don't work, but exacerbate the problem. Cities such as Detroit and Chicago are sobering examples of the urban plight perpetuated by the failed social programs of the left over the past fifty years.

The modern left has essentially lost its mind, degenerating from classical liberalism (which virtually mirrors modern right-wing libertarianism) into a post-modern potpourri of agendas that derive from classical and cultural Marxism. These include, but aren't limited to, anti-capitalism, political correctness, censorship of the right, and oppressor/oppressed power politics (which focus on class, gender, and racial distinctions). Fundamentally, the modern left is about authoritarian social engineering enforced by a quasi-fascist Big-Brother State.

The "Right-Wing" Solution

If modern left-wing politics, which forcefully and violently sacrifices the putatively sovereign individual to the dictates of the State, isn't the political solution for Buddhists, then is "right-wing" politics? Not if one considers the mainstream Republican Party to represent such politics; for, in truth, their political agenda differs only marginally from that of the Democrats. A true right-wing, or true Republican, agenda would be about reestablishing America as a true constitutional republic, wherein the constitutional rights of individuals have primacy over, rather than being subordinated to, the dictates of mob-rule democracy, wherein the brainwashed masses are able to vote them away.

In my opinion, the sociopolitical ideology that best reflects Buddhist ethics is right (or right-wing) libertarianism, which subscribes to the credo of self-ownership and the non-initiation of force. This credo or ethos perfectly meshes with the Buddha's vision of personal, interpersonal, and social morality, exemplified by his five precepts. Although libertarianism (which developed in the 1950s) is often categorized as "extreme right-wing," in reality, it closely resembles nineteenth-century classical (or neo-classical) liberalism, as opposed to modern social (progressive) liberalism.

Integral Dialectical Politics

I think the best way to explain the relation between right-wing libertarianism and left-wing social liberalism is via Hegelian dialectic, wherein the former (which represents the pole of individualism/capitalism) is the thesis, and the latter (which represents the pole of statism/socialism) is the antithesis. Because individualism/capitalism *subsumes* statism/socialism (meaning the former allows for the latter, but not vice-versa), the synthesis that results is an individualist/capitalist system that *sublates* (or subordinates but preserves) the State and allows for *voluntary* collectivism. In other words, in a moral, or "integral," society, the State still exists, but its function is limited to providing national security and protecting and preserving individual rights (including property rights).

Voluntary socialism or collectivism is fine. In an individualist-capitalist system, individuals can freely form communes or collectives if they so desire. But in a statist-socialist system, you cannot set up a John Galt-type capitalist community that is independent of the State. Big Brother will insist on regulating your town and taxing your townspeople.

The most persecuted minority is the individual, and the only social system that frees individuals from the dictates of special interest groups (which typically seek to divide and conquer through the weapons of class, gender, and racial distinctions) is *laissez-faire*, or free-market, capitalism. Free-market capitalism is based on the "trader principle," wherein independent agents voluntarily, rather than coercively, agree to exchange goods, services, and monies. This social system is the only one that morally coheres with the Buddha's five precepts and prescribed practice of right livelihood.

If "liberal" (really liberal-fascist) special-interest groups want to implement their social-engineering programs (which amount to dictatorial theft and control), instead of doing so through the agency of the domineering State, they should do so by setting up their own private Marxist or quasi-Marxist collectives and communes, rather than by forcing those of us true to Buddhist principles to participate in their socialist agenda.

The Evils of Democratic Governments

More than coincidentally, perhaps, while seated on the john during a bathroom break in the midst of writing this article, I just happened to grab a book, *The Tibetan Book of the Great Liberation* by W. Y. Evans-Wentz, from a box of many, open it to a random page, and see the apropos quote below. I took this as a sign that I was to include it in my article, so here it is:

> Plato, the greatest of Greek Sages, spent many years in an attempt to define Justice, or what the Hindu Sages call *Dharma*. He recognized the evils of democratic governments, wherein it is not the right, or justice, which always prevails, but the will of the philosophically untrained vulgar majority; and that it is fallacious to assume that the minority are always wrong. It is with these conditions in view that the *Gurus* teach that the great man is he who differs in every thought and action from the multitude. Accordingly, it has ever been the lone pioneers of thought, the sowers of the seed of new ages, the Princes of Peace, rather than the Lords of War, and the minorities (who may be the disciples of the Sages), that have suffered martyrdom and social ostracism at the hands of the majority, who impose their standards of good and evil upon the helpless minority.
>
> It is therefore very unwise to accept without question, as is nowadays customary in many modern states where sound moral principles prevail, the verdict of the people, whether expressed by a jury in a court of law or through the ballot box, as to what is justice, right or wrong, good or evil. So

long as mankind are more selfish than altruistic, the majority are unfit to dominate the minority, who may be much
the better citizens. As both Plato and the Wise Men of the
East teach, the democratic-majority standard of judgment
as to what is moral and immoral conduct is unreliable.

The fundamental point that well-meaning Buddhist Democrats need to grok is that, in a moral society, the majority has
no right to vote away the sacrosanct rights of the individual, and sacrifice him or her to the normative dictates of the
collective. For example, the government should not be able
to outlaw drugs, gambling, prostitution, and other victimless
"crimes." It should not be able to force individuals to buy med-
ical insurance, pay income tax, or get vaccinated. Those who,
a la Hillary Clinton, believe that "it takes a village" should realize that participation in the "village" must be voluntary, not
compulsory. This is so because America, first and foremost, is
a constitutional republic, and only secondarily a democracy,
which means that the democratic (voting) process should be
limited to electing officials and representatives, and should not
infringe upon the constitutional rights of citizens. When Buddhist Democrats understand this, and its relation to what the
Buddha taught regarding ethics, they will understand Right
Politics.

CHAPTER TEN

Electrical Flesh, Electrical Bones

[Note: This chapter is excerpted from my book *Electrical Christianity*.]

The Zen of Electrical Spirituality

Can you explain real meditation from an electrical energetic perspective? I've been a Zen practitioner for a long time, and I'd like to get a better understanding of my practice.

There are two major schools of Zen Buddhism—Rinzai and Soto. I predict that a third one will emerge in the future: Electrical Zen. It will emerge for one reason: Neither Rinzai nor Soto accounts for the electrical-like Energy (or Power) of spiritual life. Therefore, the door is wide open for a sharp Zen teacher to integrate the Holy Spirit into Zen.

In reality, the Holy Spirit, the *Sambhogakaya* in Mahayana Buddhism, is already one-third of the Buddhist Trinity—*Dharmakaya*, *Sambhogakaya*, and *Nirmanakaya*—but Zen, a reductionist, void-worshipping religious tradition, doesn't bother to acknowledge it. I speak knowledgeably about this, because I studied and practiced Zen for years.

So Zen needs to convert to Electrical Christianity?

No, Zen needs to convert to Electrical *religion*. The word religion is derived from the Latin word *religare*, which means to bind back to the Source. In reality, there is only one true religion or religious practice—Divine Communion. Divine Communion (called *Atiyoga* or Dzogchen in Tibetan Buddhism) is simply the yogic practice of yoking one's Soul (or *Nirmanakaya*) with the Spirit (or *Sambhogakaya*) in order to realize the timeless, spaceless God (or *Dharmakaya*).

The term Zen (*Ch'an* in Chinese) is derived from *Dhyana* (Sanskrit), which means meditation. And if Zen wants to promulgate the highest form of meditation, then it must acknowledge the practice of Electrical Spirituality (or Plugged-in Presence) as the direct, definitive way to the unborn, luminous Now.

What about the practice of koans (*intense meditative focus on confounding, paradoxical questions*)?

Original Zen meditation was all about letting go and detaching. If you read the early Chinese *Ch'an* Classics, such as *The Sutra of Hui Neng* and *The Zen Teaching of Huang Po*, all you encounter are endless directives to empty your mind, to cease grasping hold of concepts. But just surrendering or letting go, as I often point out, is an exclusive, reductive, low-energy practice, lacking the *consciousness-force*, or *spiritual voltage*, that a disciple needs to "break through" to the "Other Side."

Because "declutching" alone is not an integral practice, the Rinzai school of Zen instituted the ultra-yang practice of *koans* to counterbalance the yin practice of self-emptying. But the mentally violent, self-torturous practice of *koans*, which Zen masters liken to "trying to smash one's fist through an iron wall," is unnecessary for a disciple who practices Plugged-in Presence, which *naturally* generates even more consciousness-force than *koan* meditation.

Plugged-in Presence, Holy Communion, generates maximal consciousness-force because it *is* consciousness itself plugged directly into the Source. Consciousness (or presence) + oneness = maximal consciousness-force. If Zen didn't devote itself to denigrating man's conceptual faculty, it would have figured out this en-Light-ening formula a long time ago.

Why doesn't Zen acknowledge the Holy Spirit?

Because Zen philosophy derives essentially from Madhyamaka and the *Prajnaparamita Sutras*, which reduce everything to emptiness. Thus, any experience of any "object," even the Holy Spirit, or *Sambhogakaya*, is to be immediately voided. This anti-mind approach precludes Zen practitioners from understanding the trinitarian basis of spirituality and the role of Spirit in the en-Light-enment process. *Bodhicitta*, which means En-Light-ened Consciousness (or Conscious Light), is an important Mahayana Buddhist term, but Zen aficionados stare blankly at you when you mention Light-Energy, or Spirit-Power, as half of the Buddhahood project. The Mahayana Buddhist Trinity (*Dharmakaya, Sambhogakaya, Nirmanakaya*) mirrors the Christian one (Father, Holy Spirit, Son), but Zennists steadfastly ignore the *Sambhogakaya*, which would be like Christian mystics dismissing the Holy Spirit.

Zen Flesh, Zen Bones

In the Ten Ox Herding Pictures [Google for various interpretations], is the ox a metaphor for the Sambhogakaya, *the Holy Spirit?*

Yes. A disciple tames the wild bull, the *Shakti*, by becoming one with it. When the Zen disciple can indefinitely "ride" the now docile ox, he is well on his way to realizing his Buddha-nature. Some interpreters of these pictures consider the ox to represent one's Buddha-nature, but one's Buddha-nature can never be an object; it can only *be* the pure Subject. But when the empirical subject, the ego-self, unites with the Great Object, the reflected Light-Energy of the One Mind, then he experiences his Buddha (or Self)-nature.

How about the thirty-two marks of a Buddha?

The thirty-two marks pertain to the physical characteristics caused by the *Sambhogakaya*, the Holy Spirit. The pressure, or force-flow, of the Divine Power literally transfigures the body, leaving common, recognizable effects. It's as if you start out spiritual life as a block of stone, and God, via his *Shakti*, "carves" you into a masterpiece with specific, identifiable characteristics.

How about Zen flesh and Zen bones?

Figuratively speaking, flesh represents the *Sambhogakaya*, the *fullness* or richness of the drawn-down Supernal Efflux. Bones represent *emptiness*. When a Zen disciple's self-emptying pulls down the *Sambhogakaya*, suffusing his "bones" with Light-Energy, then the union of Flesh and Bones produces Marrow, the penetrating realization of the *Dharmakaya*, the integral Truth Body that is God.

It sounds very intense.

It is. It's as if you're being cooked alive in the purgatorial Fire of God. In the Divine Cauldron, all distinctions melt into a single Intensity, and that Intensity is the very Force of Being. Once you're sufficiently "cooked," you "cool down" and rest in "the Bright," the blissful, radiant Light of Being.

There's no way to bypass the Fire?

As Adi Da put it, "The Fire must have its way. There is no Light without Fire... That is the Law."

Electrical Religion

Can you elaborate more on electrical religion and explain the energetic process of en-Light-enment?

First, a disclaimer: I have not cut the Sacred (or Mystic) Heart-knot, and thus I am not fully En-Light-ened. Consequently, my explanation will be provisional, not definitive. Nonetheless, I am an advanced meditator, and I regularly rest in, and *as*, the Heart (or Buddha) for protracted periods, and constantly channel intense *Shakti*, or Spirit-Power. Furthermore, I am blessed/cursed with an ultra-sensitive psycho-physical vehicle

that deeply feels, and enjoys/suffers, the effects of this electrical-like spiritual, or *Kundalini*, Energy. Therefore, I am able
to describe this process as few others can. If I weren't able
to feel this Power (or Energy) and its Ohm's Law (or elec-
tric-current)-like relationship to Presence (or Consciousness)
and Poverty (or self-emptying), I wouldn't have been able to
originate and develop my Electrical Spiritual Paradigm.

The core of my natal astrology chart (Scorpio Rising, with
five planets in Cancer in the eighth house, including the Sun
closely conjunct Uranus) signifies a karmic "destiny" (or extreme tendency) to profoundly, though painfully, experience
Kundalini, Mother *Shakti*; and the rest of my chart (particularly
Jupiter in Aries in the fifth house and Neptune in Libra in the
eleventh house, opposite each other and squaring my eighth
house Cancer stellium) indicates a powerful desire to disclose
and disseminate my *Shakti*-related insights. Eventually, I will
write an autobiography detailing my fifty-year "battle" with
the Serpent Power, the "Coiled One" called *Kundalini*.

Now for the elaboration. When a yogi's conscious (plugged-
in) presence is sufficiently intense (or unobstructed), the force
(or pressure) that it generates awakens *Kundalini* (the dynamic
power of the Divine). The "lower *Kundalini*" is initially experienced as intense energy rising up from the base of the spine to
the crown. Eventually, this uncoiling, upward-rushing energy
becomes permanently "polarized" toward the crown, and the
periodic experiences of "rising ascent" subside. The yogi then
experiences the energy as a constant upward force, as a cur-

rent flow whose intensity varies according to his state of con-sciousness (meaning the consciousness-force, or voltage, he is generating, or the resistance he is releasing by self-emptying). The current's upward, "outward" pressure is particularly felt in the neck and the back of the head. It's as if the energy is seeking to escape from the "cage" of the physical.

The *ascended* spinal *Kundalini* leads a yogi to intense, absorptive *samadhis* (states of blissful, locked-in engrossment), but it cannot free him; only the "higher *Kundalini*" can. The higher *Kundalini*, the Holy Spirit, is the *descending* half of the Great Circuit, or Cur-rent, of the Divine. Whereas the lower *Kundalini* can be described as the "pushed up" power of *becoming spiritual* (which is the result of the yogi's own efforts), the higher *Kundalini* is the "pulled-down" Power of *Being Spirit-full* (which stems from Grace, the Blessing Flow from above). A smart yogi doesn't even involve himself with attempting to raise the lower *Kundalini*; instead, he simply focuses on connecting to the higher *Kundalini*, the Holy Spirit, and allowing its Light-Energy to free, or en-Light-en, him.

The higher *Kundalini*, called *Shaktipat* in Hindu Kashmir Shaivism, descends down the frontal line of the body to the Sacred (or Mystic) Heart-center. The Heart, the immanent, indwelling Source, or Soul, functions like a vacuum cleaner, sucking the Spirit (as a current) down into itself. This "pulling" action of the Heart can be strongly felt in the third-eye area of the forehead. One's head can even violently jerk and twist from the force of this pulled-down Power, or "Spirit-invasion." When the Spirit-current reaches the Heart-center, the yogi experiences radiant warmth in the area just to the right of the center of his chest, and for a time, he abides in the blissful feeling of Being, as *Shakti* and *Siva* "dance" together in his irradiated Soul.

The descending Spirit-current doesn't stop at the Heart-center. Its presence, or pressure, can also be felt below it. For example, when I meditate, my solar plexus spontaneously contracts in response to the current. Likewise, the muscles along my spinal line and neck automatically tighten when I do my spiritual practice. I've been hooked up to a biofeedback machine with electrodes attached to my back and neck muscles. When I began to meditate, to utterly let go, my heart rate slowed, my blood pressure dropped, and, incongruently, my muscles contracted, sending the tension needle on the machine's meter to and beyond its highest reading, where it stayed as long as I maintained my disposition of effortless awareness. The doctors and technicians were flabbergasted. They had never seen the needle pulled to the end marking of the tension meter before, and they had no explanation for what they had witnessed. When I started talking about the *Kundalini*, their eyes glazed over, and I realized "modern" medicine wasn't ready for the "Coiled One."

Wow! Why does Kundalini *make your muscles contract?*

Muscles contract when exposed to an electric current, and the fact that mine contract in response to the Spirit-current led me to the correlation between electricity and spirituality. Then I started thinking about Ohm's Law and noticed that it seemed to apply to my conscious *presence* (as voltage), my ego *absence* (as ohms), and the Spirit-current (as amperage). It was a perfect dialectic, with *presence* as the thesis, *absence* as the antithesis, and the Spirit-current as the synthesis. And because of my background in spiritual philosophy, I was able to tie it in with the mystical teachings of the major religions—Christianity, Buddhism, Hinduism, and Judaism.

How does Kundalini *relate to Self-realization?*

Kundalini is the Self—in its dynamic phase or dimension. When the *Kundalini* is utterly free (or unconstricted), so is the Self. Ramana Maharshi, the great Hindu sage, said *Kundalini* is just another name for the Self. Just as the flames of a fire cannot be separated from the fire, the *Kundalini* action of the Self cannot be separated from the Self, one's Divine Beingness.

A Brief Theory of Electrical En-Light-enment

Can you explain the entire electrical en-Light-enment process relative to the body? You've described the descending and ascending currents, but I'm still not clear on how they relate to Light. All you've talked about are currents.

Again, this is provisional and basic, not definitive and detailed. It's based on my own spiritual experience, what I've read, and speculation. In the future, I expect great yogi-scientists to devote their lives to demystifying the physics and superphysics involved in the "en-Light-enment of the whole body" process. But for now, I hope my undeveloped thesis proves somewhat "enlightening."

When I view the body from an electrical spiritual perspective, I think of the Heart-center (or Soul-locus) as the source, or "battery," of a circuit, with the ascending and descending currents passing through, and infinitely beyond, the brain. The brain/mind functions as a "load" (a psycho-physical mechanism of resistance) that obstructs the circuit's current flow, causing the buildup of tension or pressure in the head and neck that advanced meditators typically experience. In an En-Lightened being, the brain/mind "load" has been sufficiently altered or reduced, so as to allow the brain to function like a super light bulb, which emits a nimbus of light, or halo, which "hovers" above the crown.

Now a caveat: Even if this "battery model" is a reasonable facsimile of the Soul-Spirit nexus in a human being, an important distinction between the two must be made: Unlike the "battery model," the human Soul-Spirit is conscient and sentient; it is a knowing and feeling "entity." In other words, en-Light-enment of the bodymind can never be reduced to a "mechanical" or "scientific" description, no matter how accurate and elegant it may be.

When you talk about the brain/mind being a "mechanism of resistance," are you saying that thoughts impede the flow of the current through the brain?

That is correct. Thoughts modify and "shrink" consciousness, *contracting* it into a series of limited and bound states of consciousness. When consciousness (or voltage) is contracted, so is the current (or amperage). But you're barking up the wrong tree if you try to stop thinking. The point of real spiritual life is to outshine thoughts, not suppress them. The Light irradiates them before they can "shrink" your consciousness.

Now I'll answer your question about Light. The Spirit-current, like an electric current, produces a magnetic force-field encircling it. In the case of the Spirit-current, the magnetic force-field is called Presence or Light. The ancients knew about this Spirit-current and its correlation with the radiant, magnetic force field surrounding it, but because electricity had not yet been discovered, they had no way to explain it from a scientific perspective. One of the best allusions to this Spirit/Light relationship can be found in the Gnostic text *The Secret Book of John* (translated by Stevan Davies): "The Father looked into Barbelo [the pure Light surrounding the Invisible Spirit] ... He stood in the Spirit's presence, and it was poured upon him."

Does the magnetic force-field surrounding the Spirit-current come into play in a disciple's initiation?

Yes, it does. It's really a form of induction when a disciple enters the force-field of a spiritual master. In such a charged space, the spiritual "transmission," or initiation, can take place with just a glance or a touch from the master. And if the disciple has already been initiated, the master's presence serves to intensify his *Shakti* flow. For those interested in more information on the subject of spiritual induction, I recommend the book *Pathways Through to Space* by Franklin Merrell-Wolff (1887-1985).

If the Heart-center is like a battery, then it sounds like a Shaktipat *guru's functions can be likened to jumper cables, an outside power source that gets one's "spiritual engine" started.*

Good analogy. Just as it takes a threshold energy level to start a car, likewise it takes one to start one's spiritual life. When sufficient consciousness-force, either self-generated or *guru*-generated, is applied by, or to, an *aspirant*, then he is *initiated* by the Spirit. He becomes an *empowered disciple*, one who practices the Eucharistic discipline of Spirit Communion.

Jesus baptized his disciples with the power and presence of the Holy Spirit, or Holy *Ghost*; hence, he was called a *pneumatic*. But if Jesus were alive today, my guess is he would be referred to as a *spiritual electrician*, a divine Potentate, who, via his *Shakti*, "jump-starts," or baptizes, spiritual aspirants, thereby converting them to "true believers," *initiated conductors* of the Holy Spirit-current.

Beyond Ohm's Law: The Turning of the Wheel

What about the electrical power formula: P (Watts) = V (Voltage) x I (Amperage)? You haven't discussed watts relative to spirituality.

The webpage howstuffworks.com has a cool example of Ohm's Law and how it translates into the Power Formula:

The three most basic units in electricity are voltage (V), current (I), and resistance (R). Voltage is measured in volts, current is measured in amps, and resistance is measured in ohms.

A neat analogy to help understand these terms is a system of plumbing pipes. The voltage is equivalent to the water pressure, the current is equivalent to the flow rate, and the resistance is like the pipe size.

There is a basic equation in electrical engineering that states how the three terms relate. It says that the current is equal to the voltage divided by the resistance.

Let's see how this relation applies to the plumbing system. Let's say you have a tank of pressurized water connected to a hose that you are using to water the garden.

What happens if you increase the pressure in the tank? You can probably guess that this makes more water come out of the hose. The same is true of an electrical system: Increasing the voltage will make more current flow.

Let's say you increase the diameter of the hose and all of the fittings to the tank. You probably guessed that this also makes more water come out of the hose. This is like decreasing the resistance in an electrical system, which increases the current flow.

Electric power is measured in watts. In an electrical system, power (P) is equal to voltage multiplied by current.

The water analogy still applies. Take a hose and point it at a waterwheel like the ones that were used to turn grinding stones in watermills. You can increase the power generated by the waterwheel in two ways. If you increase the pressure of the water coming out of the hose, it hits the waterwheel with a lot more force and the waterwheel turns faster, generating more power. If you increase the flow rate, the waterwheel turns faster because of the weight of the extra water hitting it.

This water analogy is particularly neat because the turning of the waterwheel is akin to the turning of the Wheel (of Dharma) in Buddhism. Thus, when the Buddha initiated the first turning of the wheel at Deer Park in India to an audience of disciples, he was, in effect, transforming the electric "amperage" (or *Energy*) of the Spirit-current into the "wattage" (or *Power*) of Dharma transmission.

Although I loosely use the terms *Energy* and *Power* interchangeably, strictly speaking, they are not the same. Energy is simply the motion of something, and this motion can be chaotic: wasteful and unfocused. When energy is focused or organized, applied to a task, then it becomes power. For example, a light bulb's energy is measured in watts (or power) because the "wild" energy of the electrons in the current has been channeled into a specific task, that of making light. In the case of the Buddha, the "wild" universal *Shakti*, or Energy, was "tamed," and transformed into Dharma power, the first turning of the wheel.

There have been four turnings of the wheel in Buddhism: 1) The Buddha's original Dharma, 2) Madhyamaka's emptiness Dharma, 3) Yogacara's Mind-only (or Buddha-nature) Dharma, and 4) Vajrayana's tantra Dharma. I predict there will be a fifth turning of the wheel: Electrical Buddhism's Plugged-in Presence Dharma.

Why will there be a fifth turning of the wheel? Because each turning after the Buddha's reflects one-third of Ohm's Law, and the fifth turning, Electrical Buddhism, will integrate those three plus the Buddha's into a unified whole. The first turning of the wheel, by the Buddha himself, set the wheel in motion; the second, by Madhyamaka, emphasized emptiness (Poverty, or *Ohms*); the third, by Yogacara, accentuated Mind (Presence, or *Voltage*); and the fourth, by Vajrayana, focused on Energy (Power, or *Current*). The fifth turning will not only unify Buddhism, but also integrate it with Christianity.

Electrical Buddhism, Electrical Christianity

Is there any difference between Electrical Buddhism and Electrical Christianity?

No, they are just different names for the same practice. Electrical Spirituality subsumes both of them. There is no such thing as a Buddhist Truth, a Christian Truth, a Hindu Truth, or a Jewish Truth. There is only one Truth, and Electrical Spirituality is about realizing that Truth, exclusive of religious superstructures. It's fun to play with different Dharmas, to compare and contrast them—in fact, it's my favorite hobby—but unless you love philosophy, there is no reason for you to become a scholar. All you need to do is practice Plugged-in Presence—the Eucharist in Christianity, and Dzogchen in Tibetan Buddhism. And if you're incapable of doing this, then do mantra repetition or some other basic form of meditation until you are.

Regarding the Spirit (or *Shakti*, or *Sambhogakaya*, or higher *Kundalini*) and its electrical nature, all you need to know is that it's a current of Blissful Energy, with a magnetic force-field (of invisible but palpable Light) surrounding it. All you need to do is to connect to this Light-Energy and allow it to en-Light-en you. Be totally *present* (and plugged-in) and then utterly *absent*, so you become a *conscious, but empty*, cup, ready to receive the Gift, the poured-down Spirit, the electrical-like Bliss-current from above.

CHAPTER ELEVEN

Who Am I?

Thanks to the teachings of the iconic Indian sage Ramana Maharshi (1879-1950), Self-enquiry—finding out who one truly is—has become a popular spiritual practice among those into Hindu Advaita Vedanta. Buddhists also employ Self-enquiry as a means to Awakening, and given that we find different perspectives on the practice and the realization it yields, I think it's worthwhile to consider these differences. I'll begin my consideration with "Current Buddhist Teachings," continue with "Mid-Twentieth-Century Buddhist Teachings," and conclude with "Ramana Maharshi's Self-enquiry," which provides an in-depth analysis of Self-enquiry that is unparalleled in Buddhist literature.

Current Buddhist Teachings

I have read (and reviewed) dozens upon dozens of twenty-first-century Buddhist texts, and among those that consider the question "Who am I?" I find a common answer: emptiness. Led by a coterie of Buddhism professors and writers who promulgate Madhyamaka philosophy, the Buddhist zeitgeist now emphasizes emptiness as ultimate reality, while de-emphasizing or ignoring Mind as the same.

Professor Guy Newland, author of *Introduction to Emptiness*, is one of a number of Western scholars who promote the popular Tibetan Buddhist philosophy of Prasangika-Madhyamaka. In the next to last chapter of his book, titled *Who Am I, Really?* Newland answers "emptiness"—and when he says "emptiness," he means emptiness, for, as he writes, "Even emptiness is itself empty; that is, when one searches for the ultimate essence of emptiness, it too is unfindable. One finds only the emptiness of emptiness." Per Newland, "Emptiness—the ultimate reality—is the absence or lack of intrinsic nature."

What Newland doesn't understand is that emptiness isn't the root of one's identity; consciousness is. Emptiness can only be an object to consciousness. The perfectly "subjective" Seer of both form and emptiness is one's true identity or nature. This Seer, when disentangled from defiling obscurations, shines as the transcendental Self, awakened Awareness. Gautama Buddha said to take refuge in the Self, not emptiness.

Andrew Doshim Halaw is a Zen Buddhist monk and teacher whom I first became familiar with a few years ago when I read his five-star Amazon reviews of Red Pine's *Lankavatara Sutra* and Dan Lusthaus's *Buddhist Phenomenology*. These reviews made it clear to me that Halaw was clueless regarding Buddhadharma; and his book *Neti-Neti Meditation*, which is about awakening to one's True Nature, only confirmed what I already knew.

Like a number of Zennists, including the uber-popular Adyashanti, Halaw seeks to combine Buddhist Zen with Hindu Advaita Vedanta—and fails miserably. He rightly identifies *neti-neti* meditation (the contemplative practice of disidentifying from all that is not one's True Nature) as being common to both Buddhism and Hinduism, but after that it's all downhill for him.

Halaw's major problem is that he has been infected with what I call the "Madhyamaka virus." This spiritually deadly, quasi-nihilistic "virus" reduces Ultimate Reality—*Sat-Cit-Ananda*, or Self-Aware, Self-Radiant Being—to emptiness. According to Halaw, the Vedic "Tat Tvam Asi" (Thou Art That) means that your True Nature is "Thus," which is emptiness. Halaw writes: "There is just Thus...There is simply emptiness, or Thusness..."

Halaw, like most modern writers on the Zen-Advaita nexus, refers to Ramana Maharshi; and like virtually all of these writers, he doesn't penetrate beneath the surface of the great *jnani*'s teachings. He writes:

> Who is the one experiencing this? This is the central question in Sri Ramana Maharshi's atma-vichara or Self-enquiry —Who am I?... Where is this I that we assume exists? It is nowhere to be found.

In direct contrast to Halaw, Ramana Maharshi teaches that if you trace the spurious "I" to its Source, your mind spontaneously dissolves in the true, or transcendental, "I," whose locus, relative to the body, is two digits to the right of the center of the chest. And according to Maharshi, when the spurious "I" is undone in the Source, the Heart, the true, or transcendental, "I," the Self, or *Atman*, shines as infinite Awareness, and not emptiness, which can only be an object to the transcendental Subject, the Self-Aware Self.

Mid-Twentieth-Century Buddhist Teachings

Guy Newland and Andrew Doshim Halaw are just two examples of the many current Buddhist authors who identify emptiness as Ultimate Reality and one's True Nature. But if one examines the foremost Zen texts published in the mid-twentieth century, exemplified by John Blofeld's *The Zen Teaching of Huang Po* and Philip Kapleau's *The Three Pillars of Zen*, one finds Mind identified as both the Absolute and one's Buddha-nature, or Self. Because I devote two chapters to Huang Po's teachings in *Zen Mind, Thinker's Mind*, as an example of mid-twentieth-century Zen texts, I'll herein provide just some excerpts from *The Three Pillars of Zen*:

ROSHI: You must not strain yourself. Instead of trying to put your mind somewhere, simply concentrate on the question "Who am I?"

STUDENT: When I prostrate myself before you or before the image of the Buddha, or when I am chanting the sutra or walking, I have no inclination to ask myself "Who am I?" Is it all right not to at these times?"

ROSHI: You must ask the question at all times. While walking you must question, "Who is walking?" When prostrating yourself you must question, "Who is prostrating?"

STUDENT: Or else "Who am I?"

ROSHI: It amounts to the same thing.

STUDENT: I have several questions, but I don't feel like asking them.

ROSHI: Good! Unless you are bothered or worried by something it is better not to ask questions, for there is no end to them. They take you farther and farther away from your Self, whereas the question "Who am I?" brings you to the radiant core of your being.

STUDENT: I'm not worried about anything right now.

ROSHI: Don't separate yourself from "Who am I?" All questions will answer themselves once you realize your Self-nature... To be sure, when you have realized your Real-self, all this will make sense to you.

ROSHI: Within yourself you will find no "I," nor will you discover anyone who hears. This Mind is like the void, yet it hasn't a single spot that can be called empty. This state is often mistaken for Self-realization. But continue to ask yourself even more intensely, "Now who is it that hears?" If you bore and bore into this question, oblivious to anything else, even this feeling of voidness will vanish and you will be like a man come back from the dead. This is true realization. You will see the Buddhas of all the universes face to face and the Patriarchs past and present.

ROSHI: Thus in a sutra we read: "The Three Worlds are but One-mind, outside this Mind nothing exists. Mind, Buddha, and sentient beings are One, they are not to be differentiated."

Ramana Maharshi's Self-Enquiry

This is a redacted question/answer exchange on Self-enquiry between a student of mine and myself. I have divided it into three parts: The Heart-center and the Self, The Nuts and Bolts of Practice, and Miscellaneous Questions.

THE HEART-CENTER AND THE SELF

Q: Self-enquiry, finding out who one truly is, is a very popular spiritual practice nowadays. What are your thoughts on this practice?

A: I highly recommend Self-enquiry, particularly as it was taught by the late, great Ramana Maharshi. His teachings on Self-realization are the deepest and most detailed.

Q: How do you know that?

A: From decades of wide-ranging study, practice, and spiritual experiences. Anyone who can truly practice Ramana's Self-enquiry (which means "pulling the mind into the spiritual Heart-center," the soul-locus two digits to the right of center of one's chest, where one awakens to the Self) will concur with my assessment.

Q: What do you mean by "pulling the mind into the spiritual Heart-center"?

A: When an "initiated" practitioner (one who has awakened *Anugraha-Shakti*, the palpable force-flow of descending spiritual Energy) enquires to whom his thoughts arise, the Heart-center, which is the seat of the Self in an embodied being, literally sucks the thoughts into Itself, dissolving them. And when the mind is undone in the Heart-center, the Self spontaneously, for a time, shines forth as Consciousness-Radiance. When, in the rarest of beings, the Heart-center knot is severed by *Anugraha-Shakti* (which is the same force-flow as the Christian Holy Spirit and the Buddhist *Sambhogakaya*), the Self is realized and thenceforth shines ceaselessly as illimitable Consciousness-Radiance.

Q: You say that one's mind is pulled into and undone in the Heart-center. Where does the mind originate from, and where is it pulled down from?

A: The mind originates in the spiritual Heart-center, which contains one's "soul-matrix," or psychical seed tendencies. These karmic seed tendencies, in response to internal and external stimuli, sprout forth, concatenating into habit-energies, which "crystallize" as thought-forms in the brain. But in an "initiated" yogi, the mind (the "bundle" of one's thought-forms) is literally sucked back into the Heart-center, the Source wherefrom it originated. Moreover, in an advanced yogi, the habit-energies that sprout forth from the Heart-center can be "irradiated" (obviated by Light-Energy) before they crystallize as thought-forms in the brain.

Q: How does the practice of Self-enquiry relate to pulling the mind into the Heart-center and realizing the Self?

A: The "I" thought, which perpetuates the ego (or separate-self sense), is at the root of all one's thoughts. Self-enquiry is the practice of questioning each "I" thought as it arises. For example, if the thought "I want to eat" arises, one enquires: "Who am I?" Because no "I"—no entity or thinker at the root of the thought—can be found, the mind has no answer and is rendered silent. The uninitiated meditator's experience is simply this silence, but an advanced meditator concomitantly experiences *Anugraha-Shakti*, a force-current that pulls his attention (or "gaze") into the Heart-center. When his attention and the *Shakti* merge in the Heart-center, he spontaneously recognizes himself as the true, or transcendental, "I," the Self.

The Self, or Buddha-nature, is Being-Consciousness-Bliss (*Sat-Cit-Ananda*), not mere silence or emptiness. The Madhyamaka and Zen Buddhists who identify the answer to "Who am I?" as mere emptiness have not taken Self-enquiry to its onto-logical conclusion, which means finding out Who sees emptiness. The Self is Awareness, the Seer. Emptiness can only be an object. The Self, or Seer, is always the Subject, the true, or transcendental, "I" Who sees both emptiness and form.

Q: Why don't these Buddhists get to the Heart-center and recognize the Self, the true Buddha-nature?

A: Because they have not awakened *Anugraha-Shakti*, which is Blessing/Blissing Clear-Light Energy, the same Body, or Dimension, as the Buddhist *Sambhogakaya* and the Christian Holy Spirit. *Anugraha-Shakti* is also the same Hypostasis as the Hindu Bliss Sheath, which is the fifth and final (and therefore hierarchically most senior) sheath, or *kosha*, covering the Self, or Soul. The Self cannot be realized until *Anugraha-Shakti* unites with one's soul, or consciousness (contracted *Siva*), in the Heart-center; therefore, as long as one contemplates *Shakti* as an Object over against one's consciousness, it functions as a sheath, albeit a blissful one. When *Anugraha-Shakti* cuts the Heart-knot, it permanently de-contracts immanent *Siva* (one's bound pure Consciousness), and the Self shines forth as *Siva-Shakti*. When the Heart-knot is cut, *Anugraha-Shakti* transmutes into *Hridaya* (or Heart)-Shakti, as the Self-awakened yogi now radiates, rather than just receives, Blessing/Blissing Light-Energy.

THE NUTS AND BOLTS OF PRACTICE

Q: Do you have specific recommendations for the practice of Self-enquiry?

A: Yes. First, instead of disidentifying from the body, be present as the whole body. When you are organismically present, you are integrally present, which is the optimal *asana*, or position, from which to initiate the enquiry. Consciously feel yourself as the whole body and be present to existence as a single, undivided entity. Then begin the enquiry. Although, ultimately, you are timeless, spaceless Being, by being present *as* the whole body, you imbue your practice with consciousness-force, which will enable you to more quickly progress with the enquiry.

Whenever, in the course of practicing the enquiry, you become unsettled, briefly reassume the *asana* of being whole-bodily present. Once you feel integrally present, return to the enquiry.

Begin Self-enquiry by watching your thoughts. As soon as a thought with an "I" arises, such as "I don't want to meditate right now," enquire, "Who am I?" Or, alternatively, you can phrase the enquiry, "Who doesn't want to meditate right now?" or "To whom do these thoughts arise?"

If thoughts cease and you encounter silence or emptiness, enquire, "Who sees the emptiness?" Eventually, your practice will generate enough consciousness-force to make the emptiness "dance," to "come alive" as *Shakti*.

Periodically relax your bodymind and totally let go, being as if dead. This "unconditional surrender" is the perfect yin complement to the yang practice of intense enquiry. Alternating yin effortlessness (akin to ohms reduction) with yang enquiry (akin to voltage) is the optimal way to generate maximal *Shakti*, or Spirit-current (akin to amperage).

The way to the Self is via *Anugraha-Shakti*, the Spirit-current that is sucked into the Heart-center. And by alternating effortlessness with enquiry, you will, at some point, awaken (and thenceforth be able to evoke) *Anugraha-Shakti*, the "Flow of Grace" that unveils the Self in the Heart-center.

Q: Because this *Shakti*, or Energy, is an object to one's consciousness, just as thoughts and emptiness are, shouldn't one enquire, "Who experiences the *Shakti?*"

A: Yes, because so long as the *Shakti* is perceived as an Object (even a holy Object) apart from one's consciousness (or soul), it functions as the Bliss Sheath, the final covering of the soul. When this covering is removed, the soul shines as the Soul, the nondual Self, *Siva-Shakti*.

But the only way to "remove" the *Shakti*, the Bliss Sheath, is to merge your consciousness, or soul, with it. Therefore, even if you enquire into who perceives the *Shakti*, you will still perceive it, because, in the end, *Shakti*, being *Siva's* Energy, is inseparable from *Siva* (Consciousness itself). But when, upon Self-realization, the *Shakti* is no longer experienced as a separate Object, then the Bliss Sheath (or Body) is "removed," even though one still experiences the Bliss (or *Ananda*)-flow as a nondual extension of one's Self (or Beingness). In the State of Self-realization (or *Sat-Cit-Ananda*), Consciousness (*Cit*, or *Siva*) and Energy (*Ananda*, or *Shakti*) are One.

MISCELLANEOUS QUESTIONS

Q: You talk about "pulling the mind into the Heart-center." Does any other spiritual teacher talk about this?

A: Yes. The late Robert Adams (1928-1997), a direct disciple of Ramana Maharshi who spent a few years in Ramana's company. In Adams' book *Silence of the Heart,* he repeatedly enjoins his students to practice Self-enquiry and pull the mind into the Heart-center, located two digits to the right of the center of the chest. Ramaji, a contemporary spiritual teacher, also describes this experience in his books *The Spiritual Heart* and *Who Am I? Meditation.*

Q: I've read lots of Advaita Vedanta and neo-Advaita Vedanta books, and they don't talk about Self-realization the way that you do. Besides Adams' and Ramaji's books, can you recommend any other texts that go into esoteric detail regarding the Self-realization process?

A: Yes. Get *Talks with Sri Ramana Maharshi* (avoid the dumbed-down Inner Directions version), *Sri Ramana Gita,* and *Sat Darshana Bhashya.*

Q: I was under the impression that one simply had to stop thinking, or transcend the mind, in order to realize the Self. But you describe Self-realization as a multi-level process.

A: It's actually a multi-sheath process, because in order to realize the Self, one must "cut through," or transcend, the five hierarchically ordered (from grossest to most subtle) sheaths, or *koshas*, that encase or envelop (and veil) the indwelling Be-ing-Consciousness. In his monumental text *The Yoga Tradition*, the late Dr. Georg Feuerstein, the foremost twentieth-century authority on yoga, describes the five sheaths thus:

1. The *anna-maya-kosha*, or sheath composed of food; that is, of material elements: the physical body.

2. The *prana-maya-kosha*, or sheath composed of life force: the etheric body in Western occult literature.

3. The *mano-maya-kosha*, or sheath composed of mind: The ancients considered the mind (*manas*) as an en-velope surrounding the physical and the etheric body.

4. The *vijnana-maya-kosha*, or sheath composed of under-standing: The mind simply coordinates the sensory in-put, but understanding (*vijnana*) is a higher cognitive function.

5. The *ananda-maya-kosha*, or sheath composed of bliss: This is that dimension of human existence through which we partake of the Absolute. In later Vedanta, however, the Absolute is thought to transcend all five sheaths.

In the course of practicing Self-enquiry, a yogi (if he has not done so through other practices) awakens the "lower," or as-cending, *Kundalini*, which correlates with the *prana-maya-ko-sha*. This awakening facilitates the temporary transcendence of the "lower" mind (*manas*), the *mano-maya-kosha*. Self-enquiry itself involves the "higher" mind, the *vijnana-maya-kosha*, which enables the yogi to apperceive the Self as pure Awareness (though until he receives *Shaktipat* into the Heart-center, he cannot experience the transcendental Self, the Heart). *Shaktipat*, when experienced as bliss, equates to *Ananda-Shakti*, which functions as the bliss sheath (*ananda-maya-kosha*) when contemplated as a separate object. When, however, the bliss sheath, as the "higher," or descending, *Kundalini*, cascades down the frontal line of the body and converges with the soul in the Heart-center, it is temporarily transcended, as immanent *siva* (one's individual consciousness) and *Ananda Shakti*, for a time, become one. And when the bliss sheath, functioning as Grace (*Anugraha-Shakti*), severs one's Heart-knot, Divine Union is attained, and the Self, now free of sheaths, is realized.

CHAPTER TWELVE

Some Sayings of Huang Po

[What follows, in italics, are some excerpts from *The Zen Teaching of Huang Po* by John Blofeld and, in regular font, my comments to the excerpts.]

The Master said to me: All the Buddhas and all sentient beings are nothing but the One Mind, beside which nothing exists. This Mind, which is without beginning, is unborn and indestructible. It is like the boundless void which cannot be fathomed or measured.

The One Mind is a synonym for God, the single Being, or Existent, which has become all existents. This all-pervading Mind, or Consciousness, is shapeless and formless, hence it can be likened to the boundless void. The One Mind has become everything while not becoming anything.

The One Mind alone is the Buddha, and there is no distinction between the Buddha and sentient things, but that sentient beings are attached to forms and so seek externally for Buddhahood. By their very seeking they lose it, for that is using the Buddha to seek for the Buddha and using mind to grasp Mind.

The One Mind (or *Brahman*, or Father) is the Buddha (or *Atman*, or Christ). There is but a single Mind (or Buddha)-Stream.

Therefore, to use one's mind to seek Mind (or Buddha) is to obstruct the Stream. Real meditation is simply to coincide with the Mind (or Buddha)-Stream.

Only awake to the One Mind and there is nothing whatsoever to be attained. This is the real Buddha. The Buddha and all sentient beings are the One Mind and nothing else.

A *Sambhogakaya*-initiated yogi awakes to the One Mind, the *Dharmakaya,* by being Mind, immanently realized as one's Buddha-nature. When all becoming (or seeking after states of consciousness) ceases, then, spontaneously, such a one is being (or coinciding with) the One Mind, universal Consciousness.

There's never been a single thing; Then where's defiling dust to cling? If you can reach the heart of this, why talk of transcendental bliss?

From the nondual viewpoint, there has never been a single thing or separate entity, because all "things" are just temporary modifications or permutations of the "Thing-in-Itself," the Absolute, which has become all "things." From this radical (or gone-to-the-root) viewpoint, there can be no defiling dust to eliminate, because such dust is just as much the single Absolute (in appearance) as is the experience of transcendental bliss, which is not to be prized because it implies duality.

Those who hasten towards it [the Absolute] dare not enter, fearing to hurtle down through the void with nothing to cling to or to stay their fall. So they look to the brink and retreat. This refers to all those who seek such a goal through cognition. Thus, those who seek the goal through cognition are like the fur (many), while those who obtain intuitive knowledge of the Way are like the horns (few).

The Way to the Absolute—being nakedly present and clinging to nothing—induces the experience of falling into and through the void. Those willing to "leap" into the abyss and endure this "crossing" are rare.

The realization of the One Mind may come after a shorter or a longer period. There are those who, upon hearing this teaching, rid themselves of conceptual thought in a flash. There are others who do this after following through the Ten Beliefs, the Ten Stages, the Ten Activities and the Ten Bestowals of Merit. Yet others accomplish it after passing through the Ten Stages of a Bodhisattva's Progress. But whether they transcend conceptual thought by a longer or a shorter way, the result is a state of BEING: there is no pious practicing and no action of realizing. That there is nothing which can be attained is not idle talk; it is the truth. Moreover, whether you accomplish your aim in a single flash of thought or after going through the Ten Stages of a Bodhisattva's Progress, the achievement will be the same; for this state of being admits of no degrees, so the latter method merely entails aeons of unnecessary suffering and toil.

The realization of the One Mind results in a "state" (really non-state) of BEING, and what one is Be-ing is the One Mind, or Consciousness. This Being-Consciousness is the same Reality as Hindu *Sat-Cit-Ananda* and Buddhist *Nirvana* (defined as the "end of becoming," which implies awakening to, and as, Being). Because Being is Absolute, its realization admits no degrees. Moreover, because Being, or Being-Consciousness, is always already the case, it cannot be attained or gained anew. Rather, an awakened Buddha simply, unbrokenly abides in, and as, Mind, or Being-Consciousness.

But to awaken suddenly to the fact that your own Mind is the Buddha, that there is nothing to be attained or a single action to be performed—this is the Supreme Way; this is really to be as a Buddha. If you students of the Way wish to become Buddhas, you need study no doctrines whatever, but learn only how to avoid seeking for and attaching yourselves to anything.

Whatever can be attained can be lost. Because Buddhahood cannot be attained, but only awakened to, no action results in its realization. Hence, the Way to Buddhahood is through the cessation of all seeking and clinging.

Do not build up your views upon your senses and thoughts, do not base your understanding upon your senses and thought; but at the same time do not seek the Mind away from your senses and thoughts, do not try to grasp Reality by rejecting your senses and thoughts. When you are neither attached to, nor detached from, them, then you enjoy your perfect freedom, then you have your seat of enlightenment.

When you are directly and immediately present, and not seeking after anything, then you have assumed your "seat," or *asana*, of enlightenment, which unveils Mind, or Being-Consciousness.

This Dharma is Mind, beyond which there is no Dharma; and this Mind is the Dharma, beyond which there is no mind. Mind in itself is not mind, yet neither is it no-mind. To say that Mind is no-mind implies something existent. Let there be a silent understanding and no more. Away with all thinking and explaining. Then we may say that the Way of Words has been cut off and movements of the mind eliminated. This Mind is the pure Buddha-Source inherent in all men.

The Truth, or Dharma, is Mind, or Consciousness, which is neither mind nor no-mind. This Mind is one's Buddha-nature, or True Self.

This pure Mind, the source of everything, shines forever and on all with the brilliance of its own perfection. But the people of the world do not awake to it, regarding only that which sees, hears, feels and knows as mind. Blinded by their own sight, hearing, feeling and knowing, they do not perceive the spiritual brilliance of the source-substance.

Mind is not emptiness, but radiant, universal Consciousness, the all-subsuming Source-Substance of all existents.

If an ordinary man, when he is about to die, could only see the five elements of consciousness as void; the four physical elements as not constituting an 'I'; the real Mind as formless and neither coming nor going; his nature as something neither commencing at his birth nor perishing at his death, but as whole and motionless in its very depths; his Mind and environmental objects as one—if he could really accomplish this, he would receive Enlightenment in a flash. He would no longer be entangled by the Triple World; he would be a World-Transcender. He would be without even the faintest tendency toward re-

birth. If he should behold the glorious sight of all the Buddhas coming to welcome him, surrounded by every kind of gorgeous manifestation, he would feel no desire to approach them. If he should behold all sorts of horrific forms surrounding him, he would experience no terror. He would just be himself, oblivious of conceptual thought and one with the Absolute. He would have attained the state of unconditioned being. This, then, is the fundamental principle.

The fundamental spiritual principle is oneness with the Absolute, or Mind, while not being entangled by, nor avoiding, phenomena (the totality of existents stemming from Mind). He who is at-one with the Absolute attains the "state" (really non-state) of unconditioned Being.

Therefore it is written: 'The Absolute is THUSNESS—how can it be discussed?' You people still conceive of Mind as existing or not existing, as pure or defiled, as something to be studied in the way that one studies a piece of categorical knowledge, or as a concept—any of these definitions is sufficient to throw you back into the endless round of birth and death.

Because Mind, the single Existent, exists as all things (while not existing as anything), there is only Thusness. Because the Absolute is THUSNESS, it cannot be grasped as a separate Object, but can only be realized by coinciding with it.

Therefore is it written: 'Within the Thusness of the One Mind, the various means to Enlightenment are no more than showy ornaments.' Know only that you must decide to eschew all symbolizing whatever, for by this eschewal is 'symbolized' the Great Void in which there is neither unity nor multiplicity—that Void which is not really void, that Symbol which is no symbol.

There is only one direct means to Thusness, or Beingness, and that is Being-ness itself. Because Mind is uncreated, formless "Substance," it is symbolized as the Great Void, though it is not really void. And because Mind is Self-existing as the All, it is Thusness, or Beingness, which cannot be realized via symbols or concepts.

Bodhidharma firmly believed in being ONE WITH THE REAL 'SUBSTANCE' OF THE UNIVERSE IN THIS LIFE! Mind and that 'substance' do not differ one jot—that 'substance' IS MIND. They cannot possibly be separated. It was for this revelation that he earned the title of Patriarch of our sect, and therefore is it written: "The moment of realizing the unity of Mind and the 'substance' which constitutes reality may truly be said to baffle description.

The "Substance" of the Universe is Clear-Light Energy (the *Sambhogakaya*), which is not an iota different from Mind (the *Dharmakaya*), because it is Mind, in its Spirit-energetic form. Realizing the unity of Mind and "Substance" is tantamount to consummating the union of *Siva* (Consciousness) and *Shakti* (Spirit-Energy).

Once, when our Master had just dismissed the first of the daily assemblies at the K'aiYuan Monastery near Hung Chou, I happened to enter its precincts. Presently I noticed a wall-painting and, by questioning the monk in charge of the monastery's administration, learnt that it portrayed a certain famous monk. 'Indeed?' I said. 'Yes, I can see his

*likeness before me, but where is the man himself?' My question was re-
ceived in silence. So I remarked: 'But surely there ARE Zen monks here
in this temple, aren't there?' 'Yes,' replied the monastery administrator,
'THERE IS ONE.'*

The "One Zen Master" in Zen equates to *Siva* in Hinduism and
Adi Buddha in Dzogchen, meaning that it is the personification
of the Absolute. A spiritual master recognizes that his mastery
derives from his ability to coincide with and channel the Supreme Being, a.k.a. the "One Zen Master."

CHAPTER THIRTEEN

The Sword of Thusness

"The Sword of Thusness is a MEANS to Enlightenment; the Royal Treasury is the Bhutatathata—the Absolute regarded as the Source of all things."

—John Blofeld, in the endnotes of "The Zen Teaching of Huang Po"

The Way of Thusness

It is my contention that there is just a single direct means to Enlightenment—that of Thusness, or Beingness. And the enactment of this means, or "method," can be described as "the Sword of Thusness," because Thusness, when enacted, cuts through all that obstructs the expression of one's Buddha-nature. Thusness expresses one's Buddha-nature, which is Mind, or Consciousness, because it is the act of Be-ing Consciousness.

The following excerpts (in italics) from *The Zen Teaching of Huang Po*, which (in regular font) I elaborate upon, emphasize the Sword of Thusness (or *Bodhi*), which yields the direct apprehension of Mind.

It was for this reason that Mañjuśrī took up the Sword of Bodhi and used it to destroy the concept of a tangible Buddha; and it is for this that he is known as the destroyer of human virtues! Q: What does the Sword really signify? A: It signifies the apprehension of Mind.
— Huang Po

One's Buddha-nature is Consciousness, or Mind—and the apprehension of Mind (or Buddha) occurs spontaneously when one uses the Sword of *Bodhi* (or Thusness) to "destroy" all that is less than Mind, including concepts of Buddha and virtue.

[Student]: Knowledge cannot be used to destroy knowledge, nor a sword to destroy a sword. [Huang Po]: Sword DOES destroy sword— they destroy each other—and then no sword remains for you to grasp. Knowledge DOES destroy knowledge—this knowledge invalidates that knowledge—and then no knowledge remains for you to grasp. It is as though mother and son perished together. —The Zen Teaching of Huang Po

Huang Po clearly was familiar with the Tibetan Mahamudra. His cryptic statement "It is as though mother and son perished together" refers to the Mother Light (the *Sambhogakaya*) and the Son Light (the *Nirmanakaya*). When Mind is apprehended in its fullness, then there is just the *Dharmakaya*, the all-subsuming "Father Light," from whence the Mother (*Sambhogakaya*) and the Son (*Nirmanakaya*) derive.

Those who seek the Way must enter it with the suddenness of a knife-thrust. Full under-standing of this must come before they can enter.

Hence, though Bodhidharma traversed many countries on his way from India to China, he encountered only one man, the Venerable Ko, to whom he could silently transmit the Mind-Seal, the Seal of your own REAL Mind. – Huang Po

How does a seeker of the Way enact the Sword of Thusness? With the suddenness of a knife-thrust. He must enter the Way in a flash, directly and immediately. And prior to doing this, he must understand the nature and "mechanics" of his enactment.

The "Mind-Seal" refers to the Mahamudra, the Great Seal, Symbol, and Gesture. A mudra is a gesture, and the Great Gesture is the knife-thrust-like enactment of the Sword of Thusness. To the cognoscenti, such as the Venerable Ko, the Seal of one's Mind is transmitted in *Satsang*, direct communion with Being, usually through the form of a human medium or master, such as Bodhidharma. True *Satsang*, direct, unobstructed relationship with Being, morphs into Being-Consciousness, Mind-as-Thusness.

How does one enter the Way with the "suddenness of a knife-thrust"? Huang Po doesn't explain. The mind-emptying, non-clinging, and utter letting go that he enjoins do not translate into direct, immediate entry. What does is the true "Maha Mudra," the Great Gesture, which no extant Tibetan Mahamudra teaching, including Tilopa's famous *Song of Mahamudra*, discloses. This gesture can be described as the enactment of relationship, or true *Satsang*. As the iconic mystic

J. Krishnamurti wrote: "To be [unqualifiedly] related is to be [Mind, or Consciousness]." In other words, when relationship is direct, immediate, and unqualified, then, spontaneously, it morphs into perfect nondual Being-Consciousness, or Mind-as-Thusness.

The Heart Master Adi Da (a.k.a. Franklin Jones, Bubba Free John, Da Free John, et al.) espoused a Dharma that was all about relationship, or *Satsang*. According to Da, who called his Dharma "radical understanding," the ordinary, or un-Enlightened, man lives in a state of chronic self-contraction, which is caused and perpetuated by his avoidance of relationship (or conscious at-one-ment). In response to the self-contraction (the formation of awareness that is suffering), he seeks one remedial (and ultimately unsatisfying) state of consciousness after another. But none of these states touch the underlying self-contraction; at best, they only provide temporary fascination, distraction, and consolation. Because the self-contraction is generated by the psycho-physical avoidance of relationship, it is only the *asana* (or whole-bodily "posture") of relationship that can undo it. And it undoes it by "re-forming" contracted awareness into direct, immediate awareness, which, ultimately, shines as nondual Being-Consciousness, or Mind-as-Thusness.

Because the ordinary man's activity is the avoidance of relationship (the failure to be directly, immediately present and "plugged in"), Adi Da taught the practice of relational enquiry, which instigates one's assumption, or reassumption, of the *asa-*

na of relationship. This practice employs the enquiry "Avoiding relationship?" which functions as a prompt or cue to return one to the "stance" of relationship.

In my own case, the enquiry "Avoiding relationship?" serves as a "trigger device" that spontaneously "reshapes" my conscious-ness into the "great form" (or "mahamudra") of relationship. As such, it functions as a "knife-thrust" into the Way, the Mind-as-Thusness. Hence, though the enquiry is in the form of a question, it functions more as a goad that evokes resumption of the *asana* of relationship, meaning conscious at-one-ment, or "plugged-in presence," which, like a sword, cuts through "spiritual materialism" to yield nondual Being-Consciousness, or Mind-as-Thusness.

To the cognoscenti, "understanding" is the realization that what one is doing in almost every moment is avoiding relationship, failing to be directly "plugged-in" and present. "Radical under-standing" is simply the enactment of the *asana* of relationship, or plugged-in presence, which undercuts the self-contraction at its root and allows one to "stand" free as Being-Conscious-ness, or Mind-as-Thusness. And when, in a timeless moment, the force of one's free Consciousness severs one's Heart-knot, one awakens as a *Tathagata*, a Buddha who dwells forever more in, and *as*, *Tathata*, or Being-Consciousness.

Ramana Maharshi's way of Self-enquiry (see Chapter Eleven, "Who Am I?") has been described as "the Mountain Path" to Enlightenment. By comparison, the way of relational enquiry could be described as "the Cliff Path" to Enlightenment, for it is the steepest, straightest, or most direct, path to Being-Consciousness, or Mind-as-Thusness. For those interested in a full exposition of relational enquiry and the practice of radical understanding, I suggest Adi Da's first two books, *The Knee of Listening* and *The Method of Siddhas*. And I suggest the early editions, written under the name of either Franklin Jones or Bubba Free John.

CHAPTER FOURTEEN

The Five Ranks of Master Tozan

*T*he *Five Ranks* (a.k.a. *The Five Degrees of Tozan*) is a poem by the ninth-century Zen master Tozan Ryokan that describes the stages of Enlightenment in the practice of Zen. The poem, which consists of five stanzas, uses the interplay of the Absolute and the Relative to describe these stages. If you Google the Five Ranks, you'll find various interpretations of these cryptic stanzas. For what it's worth, here are mine:

The Relative within the Absolute

In the third watch of the night
Before the moon appears,
No wonder when we meet
There is no recognition!
Still hidden in my heart
Is the beauty of earlier days.

In Buddhism, the third of the four watches corresponds with initial spiritual awakening, meaning initiation into the "Stream," or Clear-Light continuum. In the case of the Relative within the Absolute, the "moon," meaning the mirror-like Clear Light of the Absolute, has not yet been apprehended; hence there can be no recognition of the Absolute. At this stage, one's true Self, or Buddha-nature, remains undiscovered in the Heart-center. Because the Heart, or Self, is timeless, its "beauty," or radiance, pertains to "earlier days."

The Absolute within the Relative

A sleepy-eyed grandma
Encounters herself in an old mirror.
Clearly she sees a face,
But it doesn't resemble her at all.
Too bad, with a muddled head,
She tries to recognize her reflection.

"Grandmother Zen" refers to gentle, or non-intense, Zen. So, this stanza alludes to a "sleepy-eyed," or unawakened, student who lacks the meditative wherewithal to awaken to his Buddha-nature. The "old mirror" is the timeless Clear Light, which, in the case of an advanced student, reflects his Buddha-nature back to him. At this stage of Enlightenment, unlike the first, the student is able to connect to the Clear Light, but being "muddle-headed," he fails to recognize his True Face in the Light.

Coming from within the Absolute

Within nothingness there is a path
Leading away from the dusts of the world.
Even if you observe the taboo
On the present emperor's name,
You will surpass that eloquent one of yore
Who silenced every tongue.

In order to recognize his Buddha-nature, the student must, at this stage, cease his efforts to do so. By resorting to "nothingness," or utter self-emptying, he creates a "path" to the Heart by drawing down Light-Energy into its center, which is felt-experienced two digits to the right of center of the chest. This withdrawal into the Heart-root, the "Seat of *Citta*," leads him from the "dust of the worlds," meaning the gross outer world, into the pure Silence within. In ancient China, the "taboo on the emperor's name" meant that the emperor, or those in power, could do or say whatever they wanted, while other couldn't. Hence, even if the student observes the taboo and remains verbally silent, his "Silence of the Heart" will eclipse the "silence," or "gag order," imposed by his rulers.

Arrival at Mutual Integration

When two blades cross points,
There's no need to withdraw.
The master swordsman
Is like the lotus blooming in the fire.
Such a man has in and of himself
A heaven soaring spirit.

At this rank, or degree of Enlightenment, the student, who is transitioning into a master, no longer withdraws into the silent Source within. Rather than resting in the Self, or Heart, apart from world, he now stands forth *as* the Self, or Heart, radiating its *Shakti*, or "heaven soaring spirit." With his Heart-lotus "blooming" in the Divine Fire, he employs "skillful means" to cut through the remaining obstacles to a constant state of integral Being, or Suchness.

Unity Attained

Who dares to equal him
Who falls into neither being nor non-being!
All men want to leave
The current of ordinary life,
But he, after all, comes back
To sit among the coals and ashes.

With unbroken, perfect Enlightenment attained, the new master is free of all "extremes," including those of being and not being (someone or something). With his *samskaras* now incinerated in the Divine Fire, he sits "among the coals and ashes," untouched by desires. From his "seat" as the Self, or Buddha, he selflessly engages ordinary life, Blessing and En-Light-ening the world with Heart-*Shakti*.

CHAPTER FIFTEEN

Zen and Dzogchen

If an impressive comparison of Zen and Dzogchen has been penned, I haven't encountered it. Zen masters and writers don't broach the subject of Dzogchen, while Dzogchen teachers who speak of Zen usually do so in brief, dismissive terms, typically reducing Zen to a *sutric* path whose aim is the realization of emptiness. The most extensive comparison of Zen and Dzogchen I've encountered is Dzogchen master Namkhai Norbu's text *Dzogchen and Zen*, but as my review (below) of it makes clear, this text hardly does a Zen/Dzogchen comparison justice:

> This "book"—if you can call a sixteen-page transcribed lecture a book—touches only briefly upon the differences between Dzogchen and Zen. Much more of the talk, given by Namkhai Norbu in 1981, focuses on the history of Dzogchen in Tibet, which isn't all that surprising given that Norbu's emphasis as a scholar was on the historical origins of Tibetan culture.
>
> Regarding Dzogchen and Zen, Norbu writes, "When one speaks of Zen and Dzogchen, it is obvious that these two methods are very different and not to be confused with one another." How are the two methods different? Norbu doesn't

adequately elaborate this. He just briefly equates Zen with
sutric Buddhism, meaning that it is, in his words, "a path of
renunciation, in which the aim is *sunyata* or void," which is
not the aim in Dzogchen. Norbu also differentiates Dzogchen from tantra, which he describes as "the path of transformation." To further emphasize the distinction between
Dzogchen and Zen, Norbu makes it clear that Dzogchen
is a tradition with roots independent of Buddhism; hence,
though it can be taught in a Buddhist context, it doesn't have
to be.

Norbu informs us that in ancient Tibet, a Zen teacher in the
Bodhidharma lineage had attempted to bring Zen to Tibet,
but the Tibetan Buddhists did not accept this theme and
became opposed to this teacher. The implication, of course,
is that Tibetan Buddhism and Dzogchen are superior to Zen
Buddhism.

The themes in this pamphlet are further elaborated in later
Dzogchen texts by Norbu. But if you don't mind dishing
out roughly a buck a page for a brief description of Dzogchen history and an even briefer description of Dzogchen
and how it differs from Zen and *sutric* Buddhism, then you
might appreciate this mini-book.

Norbu, in my opinion, errs by reducing Zen to a void-oriented
Madhyamaka practice. Anyone familiar with the greatest Zen
masters, such as Huang Po, knows that they emphasize the realization of Mind, or *Dharmakaya*, just like Dzogchen.

So how then does Dzogchen differ from high-level Zen, as epitomized by Huang Po's teachings? And does Dzogchen provide methodological instructions and philosophical perspectives that can be of use to Zen students? I'll now describe what I perceive to be the essential differences between these two Dharmas, then elaborate Dzogchen meditation, as I teach it, so students of the Way can make their own determinations.

The *Trikaya*

A major difference between Zen and Dzogchen is their understanding of and attitude toward the *Trikaya*, the Buddhist Triple Body (*Dharmakaya, Sambhogakaya, Nirmanakaya*). Whereas Zen deemphasizes the *Trikaya*, often to the point of ignoring it, Dzogchen emphasizes it, using it to explain en-Light-enment. Because Zen is a *sutra*-based tradition, built upon the *Prajnaparamita Sutras*, Nagarjuna's Madhyamaka, and Yogacara, it reduces everything to emptiness and/or Mind, which it conflates with the *Dharmakaya*. Hence, it has little use for the *Sambhogakaya* and the *Nirmanakaya*, which it considers superfluous to the Enlightenment project. Dzogchen, on the other hand, incorporates tantric concepts and practices that involve Energy, and sans the *Trikaya* doctrine, these cannot be properly explained and integrated.

Because Zen all but ignores the Energetic dimension of Enlightenment, Zennists have no real understanding of the *Trikaya*. I've read dozens of Zen texts over the past five decades, and not a single one satisfactorily explicates the *Trikaya*.

Heinrich Dumoulin (1905–1995) was one of the world›s leading scholars of Zen and the author of several books on the subject. Yet, in his *Zen Buddhism: A History*, long considered the standard work on the history of Zen Buddhism, he only once, in a single paragraph, elaborates on the *Trikaya*. He writes:

> The full expression of this new [Mahayana] Buddhology is contained in the doctrine of the three bodies of the Buddha, one of the central tenets of the Mahayana. This systematic ordering of diverse and contradictory aspects of Buddhist vision was given a final form at a rather late date, in the philosophical school of the Yogacara. The first of the three bodies is commonly referred to as the Apparitional Body (nirmanakaya). Later schools distinguish here between the complete apparition of the Perfected One (for example, of Sakyamuni) and partial manifestations (as in the case of the great Buddhist spiritual teachers). Second is the Enjoyment Body (sambhogakaya), the idealized, perfected form of the Buddha that invites personification (especially known and revered in this respect is the Buddha Amithabha, Jpn., Amida). Finally, there is the Cosmic Body of the Buddha (dharmakaya), which is none other than the absolute and consummate reality of the Buddha.

Dumoulin's description of the *Trikaya* reflects his spiritual ignorance. If Dumoulin, a Jesuit theologian, had understood the *Trikaya*, he'd have known that it's the same Triple Body as the Christian Trinity. The *Dharmakaya* is the "Father," the Supreme Being-Consciousness; the *Sambhogakaya* is the "Holy Spirit,"

Blessing/Blissing Clear-Light Energy; and the *Nirmanakaya* is the "Son," the immanent *Dharmakaya*.

Although Enlightenment can be described in monadic terms—as simply awakening to, and as, the *Dharmakaya*, or Mind—it is my contention that only a triadic, or trinitarian, description can adequately explain the Buddhahood project. Just as the Trinity was a necessary development in Christianity to make clear how a transcendent God becomes an immanent Son, Man, or Christ, likewise the *Trikaya* emerged in Buddhism to clarify and elaborate how unmanifest Mind translates into a manifest Buddha, or *Nirmanakaya*.

In Reality, there is only the *Dharmakaya*, which is timeless, spaceless Mind, or Consciousness. But when the immutable *Dharmakaya* "moves" as dynamic Spirit, or Light-Energy, which en-Light-ens *bodhisattvas*, transforming them into Buddhas, then it is appropriate to describe this "action" of the Absolute as the *Sambhogakaya*, meaning the *Dharmakaya* in its mode or dimension as Divine Power. And when the *Dharmakaya*, as the Blessing Power of the *Sambhogakaya*, unobstructedly radiates through a human medium, it is right to describe the En-Light-ened human vehicle as a *Nirmanakaya*.

Dzogchen Meditation

In the past half century, I have practiced and taught Vipassana, Zen, and Dzogchen meditation. And in my opinion, Dzogchen, via its core practice of *rigpa*, provides the most direct and integral form of meditation. *Rigpa* consists of two fundamental and complementary components—*trekcho* and *togal*—and when these are properly understood and implemented, en-Light-enment naturally ensues. Because *trekcho/togal* practice is best explained in a trinitarian (or "triple body") context, Dzogchen, properly, emphasizes the *Trikaya*.

What follows are question/answer exchanges on *rigpa*, *trekcho*, and *togal* between a few of my students and myself. These edited exchanges provide an essential elaboration of Dzogchen meditation, as I teach it. After the exchanges, I conclude by summarizing my view of Dzogchen for Zen students.

Rigpa: Primal Presence

Rigpa *is the prescribed practice in Dzogchen. How would you describe it?*

Rigpa is the practice of primal presence, which bestows radical (or gone-to-the-root) gnosis (or spiritual knowledge) and whole-body en-Light-enment (or Spirit-current irradiation). It is commonly described as naked or intrinsic awareness, but because one is be-ing (or attempting to be) present *as* this awareness, it is better described as direct and immediate presence.

When a yogi is directly and immediately present, the pressure of his (consciously "plugged-in") presence generates a force that wants to move. When this force begins to move as palpable, even visceral, energy, he has been "initiated" into "the awakening process." When this force is experienced in its "higher" form as descending (or "crashing-down") energy into the spiritual Heart-center (located two digits to the right of the center of the chest), he has awakened to *Dharmamegha*, the *Dharmakaya* as Heart-awakening Clear-Light Energy.

Radical gnosis (or understanding) grows from "standing under" and contemplating the *Sambhogakaya*, the Clear-Light continuum from on high. The yogi understands that his connection to the Clear Light is what en-Light-ens him; and this gnostic understanding prompts him to re-establish (or attempt to re-establish) his connection whenever he becomes aware that he has lost it. Permanent union with the Clear Light means that the yogi has acquired a Light Body. It signifies that as a fully En-Light-ened *Nirmanakaya* (or Buddha), the *Sambhogakaya* and the *Dharmakaya* have become one in, and *as*, him.

Your description of rigpa *sounds just like Hindu yoga, wherein the yogi attempts to unite with universal Spirit, which you equate with Clear-Light Energy, the* Sambhogakaya.

Yes, I equate the two, and I contend that by explaining *rigpa* and Dzogchen in non-Tibetan contexts, including that of Hindu yoga, I am furthering their understanding and dissemination.

Rigpa *is sometimes described as "knowledge of the Ground." How does the yogi acquire this knowledge?*

The Ground is Mind, universal Consciousness, or Awareness. It can only be "known" (or yogically realized) in the spiritual Heart-center (termed *Hridayam* in Hindu yoga, and *Tathagatagarbha* in Mahayana Buddhism). The only way to the Heart-center, or "Womb of Buddhahood," is through the descent of Divine Power, the *Sambhogakaya*, which is the same "Body" as Hindu *Shakti* and the Christian Holy Spirit. The descent of this Divine Power, or Light-Energy continuum, into the Heart-center "produces" the Four Visions of *Togal*, the four progressive states of realization of *Dharmata* (universal Suchness, or Beingness).

How do trekcho *and* togal *figure into your view of* rigpa?

Trekcho and *togal* are the two fundamental (and complementary) components of *rigpa*. *Trekcho* is the "consciousness" aspect of *rigpa*, wherein the yogi, applying his conscious presence like a diamond-cutter, attempts to cut through "spiritual materialism" (meaning all that is not Spirit) to get to the "Other Side," which is Spirit, the *Sambhogakaya*. *Togal* is the "conductivity" aspect of *rigpa*, wherein the yogi, who is connected to Spirit, channels, or conducts, its Light-Energy.

Trekcho: Cutting Through Spiritual Materialism

You've described trekcho *as "cutting through spiritual materialism to get to Spirit itself." Can you describe this practice in more detail?*

Trekcho, sometimes described as "breakthrough," is the practice of assuming, and maintaining, the *asana*, or "position," of direct, immediate presence. This *asana* "shapes" consciousness into a "cutting tool" that enables the yogi to "cut," or "break," through "spiritual materialism" (meaning all that is not Spirit) to get to the "Other Side," which is Spirit, the *Sambhogakaya*. Hence, *trekcho* is simply *rigpa* applied as a "cutting tool."

I'm not clear on what you mean by "direct, immediate presence"? Can you clarify it for me?

I'll explain it a couple of ways. One way to understand it is as awareness-oneness. In other words, the yogi isn't just aware, he's also plugged into the abstract whole, at-one with existence. Think of it this way: awareness is like turning a lamp on, but without plugging it in, there is no light or power. Awareness becomes plugged-in presence when one, whole-bodily, lives *as* it in relation to life. Plugging awareness, *as* embodied presence, directly into life transforms it into a penetrating force that cuts through the dross separating one from Spirit. This penetrating force of consciousness, when experienced as a dynamic "pressure," "pushes" the yogi through his dross until he "breaks through" to the "Other Side," meaning Spirit, or the *Sambhogakaya*.

A second way to explain presence is to understand it *as* relationship. In other words, plugged-in presence *is* relationship. To be directly, immediately present is to be in, and *as*, relationship. Although relationship implies dualism, when it is direct and unobstructed, it spontaneously morphs into nondual being-consciousness. And when one's consciousness (*as* relationship) is Blessed by the descent of Divine Power into the Heart-center (located, or felt-experienced, two digits to the right of the center of the chest), then one's State is that of Divine Being-Consciousness.

In my own meditation practice, I employ the self-enquiry "Avoiding relationship?" whenever I become aware that I have retracted from the *asana*, or "psycho-physical posture," of plugged-in presence. This self (or relational)-enquiry serves to instigate my resumption of the *asana* of relationship.

Trekcho is about generating the consciousness-force to "break through" to the "Other Side." And because relationship, when consciously lived, generates maximal consciousness-force (or pressure), it is the definitive *trekcho* practice.

So, relationship is the epitome of trekcho?

Yes. The *asana* of direct, immediate relationship spontaneously "organizes" one's consciousness into a penetrating force that cuts through spiritual materialism. Hence, in the words of the great spiritual adept Adi Da Samraj (1939-2008), "Relationship is the discipline."

Relationship implies relationship to something. What is one supposed to be in relationship to?

Everything and anything. Relationship can be to the abstract whole, to empty space, or to objects (gross or subtle) arising or abiding within space, including one's body and mind. Ultimately, one cuts through all of these and encounters the ultimate Object, Spirit itself. And when one's consciousness unites with Spirit, relationship morphs into nondual Being-Awareness.

Practically speaking, empty space is an ideal object for one's contemplative (or relational) focus, which is why Dzogchen emphasizes it. Basic Dzogchen practice often begins with simple "gazing into space." Once your attentional "gaze" is stabilized, you should then practice being in direct relationship to space.

What's so special about empty space as an object of contemplation?

First, it functions as a mirror that reflects your activity back to you. In the context of relationship to empty space, you can clearly and objectively view your thoughts. Most importantly, you can see and feel them as formations of consciousness that contract the field of open awareness into enclosed states of self-constriction. When you can see and feel this, your response should be to let go of the grasping mind-forms that generate the self-contraction, the "clenched fist of consciousness" that is suffering.

Secondly, empty space functions as a doorway to Spirit, the *Sambhogakaya*. When empty space begins to "dance," to come alive as "gift waves" of *Shakti*, this Blessing Power, or Clear-Light Energy, literally en-Light-ens you, outshining your thought-forms. Conducting and resting in this Light-Energy continuum is the essence of *togal*, which we'll consider after our *trekcho* discussion.

What is empty space?

It is the *Akasha*, the formless, universal Space element, a.k.a. the ether. The *Akasha*, or ether, is the primal ethereal "substance" that underlies and pervades the cosmos. It is the root element from which the four gross elements (fire, earth, air, and water) derive. Tibetan Buddhists err when they conflate emptiness or empty space with the *Dharmakaya*, which is timeless, *spaceless* Awareness. Space is a created substance or element, whereas the *Dharmakaya* is uncreated Being-Consciousness.

Interestingly, *Akash*, which is the corresponding word to *Akasha*, means "Sky" in many Indo-Aryan languages; hence, when Dzogchen students are instructed to gaze into the open sky in front of them, this is tantamount to focusing one's attention on the ether.

In Dzogchen, three different ways of thoughts self-liberating themselves are described. What can you say about this?

First off, thoughts don't self-liberate because thoughts aren't bound and in need of liberation. Liberation pertains to the self, meaning the individual or yogi. That said, the three ways of liberating oneself from thoughts described in Dzogchen are valid and represent a continuum of reduced effort. The first, or most "effortful," of the three ways is that of bare or naked attention, wherein the yogi looks directly at the thoughts, thereby dissolving them. This level has been described as "like a dew drop evaporating in the sun."

The second of the three ways is that of indirectly vanishing thoughts by neither accepting nor rejecting them. This approach, which is akin to J. Krishnamurti's choiceless awareness, involves some effort, because one must practice allowing thoughts to just be and dissolve of their own accord. This level has been described as "like snow melting as it falls into the sea."

The third, or effortless, way, is that of Self-liberation itself. When one is rested in the Self, or Buddha-nature, superfluous thoughts are spontaneously incinerated in the radiant Intensity of the Clear Light, and functional thoughts are automatically un-done as soon as they have done their work. This level has been described as "like a snake unwinding the coils of its own body."

Beyond thoughts, what are the obstructions to uniting with Spirit, the Clear-Light continuum?

Besides the mind (conscious and sub-conscious), the obstacles, or sheaths, of spiritual materialism that one must cut through include the gross, or physical, body, the subtle, or individual *pranic* (etheric), body, and, ultimately, Spirit, or the *Sambhoga-kaya*, because when it is objectified as a Dimension or Body separate from the *Dharmakaya*, it functions as a sheath that veils the Vision of *Dharmata*, the True Nature of existence.

How is one to cut through these sheaths? Simply by practicing *trekcho*, which means being directly and immediately present to, and through, whatever arises. And when the yogi's consciousness intersects the *Sambhogakaya*, the Holy Spirit, *trekcho* morphs into *togal*—contemplation of the Clear-Light continuum.

Beyond the "monkey," or discursive, mind, Dzogchen texts pay scant attention to the other sheaths of spiritual materialism, which are more deeply considered in the Hindu yoga traditions. Let's now consider the classic five sheaths that, according to Vedantic philosophy, veil the Absolute.

The first sheath (*annamaya kosha*) is one's gross, or "meat," body. This physical "vehicle" can be viewed negatively (as a temporarily animated carcass) or positively (as a temple of the Divine). Regardless of how one views the body, it has to be "cut through," or penetrated (and interpenetrated), by the "diamond" of consciousness.

The second sheath (*pranamaya kosha*) is one's vital, or subtle-energetic, body. This sheath is reflected in one's *nadis*, *chakras*, and aura. When a yogi begins to cut through the sheaths, *Kundalini* (coiled "Serpent Power") awakens, and this uncoiling Power can be felt as a pressure and movement in both the gross and subtle-energetic bodies. The practice of *pranayama*—consciously focusing on one's breathing cycle—intensifies the pressure and movement of this subtle, or etheric, energy. There can be no en-Light-enment without this cosmic-etheric energy cutting the knots in one's subtle body. But the subtle body should not be confused with the causal body, the true Spirit Body/Energy, which severs the yogi's causal (or Heart)-knot

The third sheath (*manomaya kosha*) is one's "lower" mind, one's mental habit-energies, or psychical proclivities, which generate entanglement with, and bondage to, "gross" phenomena (e.g., money, food, and sex) and "subtle" phenomena (e.g., one's judgments, memories, and emotions). When one's mind (*citta* functioning as *manas*) dwells upon and grasps hold of objects, gross or subtle, then one's consciousness has contracted into the activity called "lower mind." But when one's consciousness (*citta*) begins to function as *Cit* (pure Consciousness itself) rather than as *manas* (mental-formations), then one begins to cut through, or transcend, the "spiritual materialism" generated by this sheath.

The fourth sheath (*vijnana kosha*, a.k.a. *buddhi*) is one's "higher" mind, or ascertaining intelligence, which enables one to perceive the self-contracting nature of his mind (*manas*). The "higher mind" not only enables the yogi to recognize the binding nature of his mental activity, it also instigates his transcendence of the mind by informing him to live from the "position" of Consciousness Itself (*Cit*) rather than to be enmeshed in self-entangling mind-forms.

The fifth, and final, sheath (*anandamaya kosha*) is the causal body, which, in and of itself, is not a sheath, but pure Spirit, the Energetic Dimension of the Absolute, a.k.a. the *Sambhogakaya*. But because the yogi cannot transcend subject-Object entanglement with this Light, or Bliss, Body until this Body itself, functioning as Blessing Power, or Grace (*Anugraha-Shakti*), severs his Heart-knot (*Hridaya-granthi*), it is considered a sheath from the viewpoint of the path.

Can you summarize what you've said so far about trekcho *as a cutting tool?*

Trekcho is the "tool" the yogi uses to cut through spiritual materialism to get to Spirit, the "Other Side." When his consciousness assumes the *asana* of relationship (or awareness-oneness), it morphs into a diamond-like cutting tool that penetrates (and interpenetrates) the first four sheaths until it encounters Spir-it, Divine Power. Then, in turn, it penetrates and is penetrated by Spirit itself, which the yogi receives as *Shaktipat*—down-poured Blessing Power. When this Spirit-Power, or *Shakti*, cuts the yogi's Heart-knot, it permanently unites with his con-sciousness or "soul" (*citta*), and frees it for all eternity. At this Divine "juncture," spiritual materialism has been cut through forever by the yogi, the "diamond cutter" par excellence.

Trekcho is *rigpa*, direct naked presence, applied to "breaking one through" to the *Sambhogakaya*, the Spirit-current. *Rigpa* as *trek-cho*, or "plugged-in" presence, "organizes" one's consciousness into an adamantine intensity that penetrates through the ob-structions to the Spirit-current, which one then contemplates, conducts, and unites with in *togal*. Plugged-in presence is a syn-onym for direct, immediate relationship. When relationship is unobstructed, one's consciousness intersects the *Sambhogakaya,* the radiant Spirit-current, or Clear-Light continuum, and one proceeds, progressively, through the Four Visions of *Togal*.

In Tilopa's *Song of Mahamudra*, Tilopa sings, "The void needs no reliance, Mahamudra rests on naught." Likewise, the void, or empty space, needs no reliance in Dzogchen but is a recom-mended object of contemplation because it provides an ideal "backdrop" or "something" to focus one's attention on. This is the case because thoughts tend to dissolve when one "stares into space." And as the *pranically* charged ether, the void serves as a direct portal to Spirit. A recommended adjunct practice is to consciously breathe (or inhale and exhale) the empty space, which, in an "initiated" yogi, suffuses his body with *prana* and intensifies his connection to space and Spirit. A final word on empty space: One can freely gaze into it, but real *trekcho* practice is to be in relationship to, and through, it, to the "Other Side," a.k.a. the *Sambhogakaya*.

Togal: Conducting the Clear-Light Continuum

What can you say about togal? *Is it a separate practice from* trekcho, *or just an extension of it?*

It's an inseparable extension of *trekcho*, and the iconic Dzogchen master Longchen Rabjam agrees. He writes, "People who cling to Thregchod [*Trekcho*] and Thodgal [*Togal*] separately and practice accordingly are similar to a blind person examining forms."

Until a Spirit-initiated yogi is fully Enlightened, there will be times when he cannot practice *togal* (directly connecting to the Clear-Light continuum, or Spirit-current) and must resort to *trekcho* (cutting through spiritual materialism to get to the "Other Side," which is Spirit, or the *Sambhogakaya*). Viewed from the perspective of Hindu tantra, *trekcho* can be likened to *Satsang* (communion, or attempted communion, with the Divine), while *togal* is akin to *Shaktipat* (directly receiving Divine Power).

Common definitions of *togal* include "leap over," "direct crossing," "direct vision of Reality," and "spontaneous presence." "Leap over" and "direct crossing" imply that the yogi bypasses *trekcho* and immediately connects to and contemplates the Clear-Light continuum. "Direct vision of Reality" and "spontaneous presence" describe this connected state. For until the yogi's consciousness converges with the Clear Light, he cannot experience a "direct vision of reality" and enjoy a state of "spontaneous presence."

An advanced yogi directly and immediately "leaps over" spiritual materialism to Spirit itself, the "Other Side." Once he "leaps over" to the "Other Side," and "locks-in" to the Spirit and begins to channel it, his infused contemplation (which allows him to rest in the Spirit-current) can be described as a state of *samadhi*-like "spontaneous presence."

Isn't your description of togal *dualistic, and therefore contrary to the nondual Dzogchen approach?*

Complain to Longchen Rabjam! He describes Dzogchen as the "union of the ultimate sphere and intrinsic awareness." The fact is, Di-"vine" yoga, which involves the union of the "vine" of consciousness (or awareness) and the "vine" of Spirit (or Clear-Light Energy), is a nondual practice. This is so because intrinsic awareness and Light-Energy are only *apparently* separate. But from the perspective of the *Maya*-enmeshed yogi, who must, literally, cut through the sheaths that prevent his nondual realization of intrinsic awareness and the Clear Light as One, this separation is an ontic reality.

Can you describe the stages of Enlightenment engendered by the infusion of Light-Energy in togal?

There are "Four Visions" (or four stages) of *togal*, and Dzogchen teacher Namkhai Norbu describes them thus:

> The first of the Four Visions of Thodgal [Togal] is called the "Vision of Dharmata" (or "nature of reality") and the second vision is the further development of the first. The third is the maturation of it, and the fourth is the consummation of existence.

As Norbu's description makes clear, there aren't four separate visions; there is a single "vision" that intensifies or matures until it culminates in the realization, or "Vision," of *Dharmata*, universal Suchness, or Beingness.

I contend that true *togal* is channeling/contemplating the *Sambhogakaya*, a.k.a. the *Dharmamegha* (or Dharma Cloud). I also contend that this practice is not unique to Dzogchen, but can be found in other traditions. For example, in Mahayana's Ten Stages (*Bhumis*) of a *Bodhisattva's* Enlightenment, the final four stages are classified as "pure," and the first six stages as "impure." This is so because the final four stages, which are akin to *togal's* Four Visions, involve contemplation of the unborn Clear Light, which is "Purity" itself.

When the descent of the *Dharmamegha* (or Dharma Cloud) into the spiritual Heart-center (*Tathagatagarbha* in Mahayana, *Hridayam* in Hinduism) is complete, meaning that one's Heart-knot has been cut, then *Bodhicitta*, or Buddhahood, is attained. *Bodhicitta* means Conscious Light, or En-Light-ened Consciousness, and signifies the permanent union of one's consciousness (*citta*) with Clear-Light Energy, the *Sambhogakaya*, or Dharma Cloud. As such, despite claims to the contrary by parochial Buddhists, this is the same realization as in Hindu yoga, wherein the yogi's individual consciousness permanently unites with universal Spirit, or *Shakti*.

When the Heart-knot is cut in the *Tathagatagarbha*, the yogi, or *bodhisattva*, attains *Bodhicitta* and becomes a *Tathagata*, a Buddha who dwells forever more in, and as, Suchness, or Beingness, called *Tathata* in Mahayana Buddhism, and *Dharmata* in Dzogchen.

Longchen Rabjam defines *togal* as "resting in the continuum of the radiance of Awareness." This is tantamount to a Christian mystic channeling the Holy Spirit, a Jewish mystic receiving the Supernal Influx, and a Hindu yogi conducting the *Shakti*-current. Again, Dzogchen is not superior to other forms of pure mysticism; it's just "packaged" and "marketed" to convince its followers and practitioners that it is.

Can you speak more on the Four Visions?

Again, they simply refer to the depth (or intensity and fullness) of the descent of the *Dharmamegha*, the down-poured *Sambhogakaya*. The "Clear" Light is clear, meaning that it can't be seen. Rather, it is felt-intuited. "Seeing" the Light is just a figure of speech. Yes, one can see all kinds of things (especially in the dark), including *thigle* (spheres of rainbow light), but this is a manifestation of Clear-Light Energy, and not the unmanifest Clear Light itself. One attains a Light Body when the fourth "Vision" is consummated, but any "rainbow" manifestation is superfluous to this attainment.

Namkhai Norbu (who passed in 2018) and current Dzogchen teachers do not agree with my view of *togal* and the Four Visions. Instead, they shroud the practice of *togal* in secretive mystery, holding it out as the proverbial carrot in front of the "donkey" (meaning the naive disciple). Regarding *togal [thodgal]*, Norbu writes: "This practice is genuinely secret, and it is not appropriate to give more than the most basic description of it here. This is not the same as an instruction for practice. Thodgal is found only in the Dzogchen teachings." According to Norbu, (who doesn't elaborate beyond this), "Through the development of the Four Lights, the Four Visions of Thodgal arise, and working with the inseparability of vision and emptiness, one proceeds until the realization of the Body of Light is attained."

My response to Norbu (and Dzogchen teachers who share his *togal* view) is: Real *togal* has nothing to do with "secret" teachings (which typically involve visions that one attains while gazing at the sun or meditating in dark caves or rooms). It has nothing to do with visual experiences of *thigle* or any lights correlated with the Four Visions. The Four Visions, in fact, are "visions" of the Clear Light, which is invisible, and can only be felt-experienced. Visions of (manifest) colored lights that one might experience in *togal* are not experiences of the (unmanifest) Clear Light itself.

To mystics steeped in the Esoteric Perennial Philosophy, the Four Visions can be likened to the Four *Jhanas* in original (or Pali) Buddhism, the seventh to tenth *Bhumis* (or stages) of a *bodhisattva's* en-Light-enment in some Yogacara schemas, and the four levels of Grace in Christian mysticism.

In esoteric Yogacara, the seventh to tenth stages of the ten stages of a *bodhisattva's* en-Light-enment reflect the progressive intensification of the descent of the *Dharmamegha* (or Dharma Cloud). The full descent of the *Dharmamegha* (or *Sambhogakaya*) into the *Tathagatagarbha* (or Sacred Heart-center) yields *Bodhicitta*, or *Tathata,* which is the same Divine "State" as *Dharmata*. My guess is that the Dzogchen tradition "appropriated" the final four stages of a *bodhisattva's* en-Light-enment, "dressed it up" as a visionary yoga, and "privatized" it as "secret *togal* teachings."

With regard to Christianity, I contend that the First Vision correlates with Baptism, the Second with Confirmation, the Third with Sanctifying Grace, and the Fourth with Divine Union/Beatitude. Each of these "Visions" stems from the progressive intensification of the descent of the Holy Spirit, or *Sambhogakaya* (which renowned Buddhist scholar Christmas Humphreys defined as "Divine Power"), until consummating Divine Union, or Supreme Beingness, is realized. *Dharmata* is a synonym for Beingness; and the union of the "vine" of one's soul (or consciousness) with the "vine" of Spirit, or the *Sambhogakaya*, "produces," or unveils, Di-"vine," or Supreme, Beingness, the Fourth Vision of *Dharmata*. This is coincident with attaining a Light Body, because the *Sambhogakaya* is the Light Body.

In Dzogchen, the Third Vision is said to reveal a full, though not yet permanent, vision of the *Dharmata*. This vision correlates with Sanctifying Grace in Christianity, which signifies the attainment of sanctuary in the Sacred Heart-center (equivalent to the Heart-Essence in Dzogchen). When Grace, the Descent of the Holy Spirit, or *Sambhogakaya*, intersects the contracted *Nirmanakaya* (or immanent *Dharmakaya*) in the Heart-center, de-contracting it, the yogi experiences *Dharmata*, Di-"vine" Beingness, as the True Nature of existence. Sans the attainment of this Third Vision of *Dharmata*, a yogi cannot "crack the code" of Buddhadharma.

Can you describe togal *practice in more detail?*

As I see it, there are three variations of *togal* practice: one yin, one yang, and one neutral. The yin practice is that of being an empty container that consciously receives, and is filled, to one degree or another, with the Blessing/Blissing Light-Energy of the down-poured *Sambhogakaya*. The yang practice is that of consciously converging with the *Sambhogakaya*. And the neutral practice is that of resting in the Light-Energy continuum. In a single meditation session, an advanced practitioner can, more than once, cycle between these three variations. Because spiritual contemplation is an art, the yogi, employing "skillful means," must determine which variation(s) of *togal* to emphasize in a given session.

Zen Meets Dzogchen

The term *Zen* derives from the Chinese term *Ch'an*, which stems from the Sanskrit term *Dhyana*, which means meditation. Hence, Zen Buddhism is simply meditation practice directed at the attainment of Buddhahood. As such, Zen is not limited to any specific practices, but can freely incorporate methods from other traditions that might aid in the quest for Enlightenment. Given this reality, there is no reason for Zen students not to experiment with Dzogchen.

Zen practice evolved over the centuries because Zen masters, through trial and error, learned what worked and what didn't for their students. For instance, early Zen in China, in accordance with the *Diamond Sutra*, its de facto bible, was all about the practice of non-clinging, the cultivation of a non-abiding mind. But at some point, it became evident that this yin practice of letting go of thoughts from moment to moment did not, for most students, generate sufficient consciousness-force to induce spiritual breakthrough. Hence, yang *koan* practice was developed, which continues to this day.

But does *koan* practice, in conjunction with non-clinging, represent the apex of spiritual practice? Not from my experience. First off, *koan* practice does not generate maximal consciousness-force, which is the goal of yang meditation. But *trekcho*, properly practiced, does, because it is about being present *as* Mind, which generates maximal consciousness-force. Secondly, yin spiritual practice—non-clinging, or utterly letting go—which naturally follows yang practice, facilitates the "pulling down" of Clear-Light Energy, the *Sambhogakaya*, which produces en-Light-enment. But because Zen, unlike Dzogchen, ignores the *Sambhogakaya*, it can't explain en-Light-enment from an energetic perspective, but only from the static viewpoint of Mind or emptiness. Moreover, because Zen doesn't account for Light-Energy, it can't make use of tantric spiritual practices, which intensify the movement of Light-Energy, or *Shakti*, which quickens en-Light-enment.

There can be no Enlightenment without Light-Energy, and though Zen does not directly describe Light-Energy, it indirectly alludes to its presence in various stories, a couple of which I'll now recount.

The first story is one I came across in William Irwin Thompson's book *Coming into Being: Artifacts and Texts in the Evolution of Consciousness*. Thompson writes:

> There is a famous tale of *koan* practice in which the Zen master looks at his student [after morning meditation] and asks him, "Have you had your breakfast?" The student answers yes, and then the master responds by saying, "Then clean your bowl."

The story's meaning is this: The Zen master can see the student's aura, so he knows that he was basking in the radiance of the Light-Energy continuum; but now that it's time to work, he can't be blissfully absorbed in it, but rather, needs to revert to self-emptying.

The second story is a popular one, rendered by Mindfueldaily. com as follows:

> A well-known professor went to visit a Zen master. As the master gracefully served tea, the professor described his ideas of Zen. The master remained quiet as the professor spoke, continuing to pour. When the tea reached the brim of the cup, the Zen master kept pouring. The tea over-flowed, spilling onto the tray, the table, and the carpet, un-til the professor could no longer stand it. "Stop!" he said. "Can't you see the cup is full?" "This is you," said the master, pointing to the cup. "How can I show you Zen, until you first empty your cup?"

The only "thing" that can fill the bowl and the cup in these two stories is Clear-Light Energy, the *Sambhogakaya*. The *Dharmakaya*, or Mind, cannot, because Consciousness can't be di-rectly transmitted and enjoyed in and of itself, but necessitates Light-Energy, the Holy Spirit, as its transmissive medium. While this is only implicitly alluded to in various Zen stories, it is made explicitly clear in Dzogchen.

To sum, even high-level Zen, as epitomized by Huang Po's teachings, does not detail the practice of conscious presence (in order to apprehend Mind), but Dzogchen, via *trekcho*, does. Moreover, because Zen does not employ the *Trikaya*, it has no way to explain en-Light-enment—how *citta* becomes

Bodhicitta; but Dzogchen, via *togal* (and its Four Visions), does. Hence, by adopting Dzogchen's "view" (or *Trikaya* philosophy) and practices (of *trekcho* and *togal*), Zen can upgrade its Dharma.

CHAPTER SIXTEEN

Future Zen

[This chapter consists of edited talks between a few of my students and myself. Some of the conversations recapitulate (while expanding upon) subject matter in the previous chapters, and some break new ground.]

Soto vs. Rinzai

Is Soto or Rinzai the future of Zen, or does a new school of Zen need to emerge for Zen to evolve to its full potential?

That's a good question, and if I hadn't (in late 2018) read a couple of contemporary Rinzai Zen texts (*Practical Zen: Meditation and Beyond* by Julian Daizan Skinner and *The Rinzai Zen Way: A Guide to Practice* by Meido Moore) that changed my mind, I would have said that an entirely new school of Zen must emerge. But given that some modern Rinzai teachers not only integrate energy practices into their Zen, but also seem open to incorporating practices from outside the Zen tradition, it's possible that Rinzai can evolve into the "Future Zen" I envisage.

What's the problem with Soto?

I think that Skinner, who is intimately familiar with both Soto and Rinzai, nails it in *Practical Zen*. He spent a decade-and-a-half as a Soto monk before he soured on the tradition and moved on to Rinzai. Why did he sour on Soto? Because he realized that the passive Soto practice of "just sitting" doesn't work for most people, that people in general need a "means of ignition" to get their spiritual life going. Hence, he turned to Rinzai and became a student and then a master in the tradition. My own Zen experience in Soto groups mirrors Skinner's, and my long-time "problem" with the practice of "just sitting," or effortlessness, led me to develop my Electrical Spiritual Paradigm (ESP), which explains why yang practices, such as *koans* and energy work, are instrumental in quickening the en-Lightenment process.

So what does Rinzai need to do to evolve into the Electrical Zen you envisage?

First off, Rinzai needs to upgrade its *koan* practices and energy work. For example, regarding *koans*, Skinner favors the question "Who am I?" He writes: "The most important koan is 'Who am I?' Everything comes from that." But Skinner, as made clear in his book, has no real understanding of this *koan* (which Advaita Vedanta calls "Self-enquiry"). And neither do his fellow Zen teachers. But if they read my article "Who Am I?" [Chapter Eleven in this book] and study the teachings of the iconic Indian Guru Ramana Maharshi [check out his texts in the Advaita Vedanta category of my Spiritual Reading List], they will be able to teach Self-enquiry on the esoteric level it is meant to be taught. The other "koan"—really enquiry—that Rinzai should emphasize is Adi Da's relational enquiry, which is detailed in his first two books, *The Knee of Listening* and *The Method of the Siddhas*. (I recommend the early editions, written under the name of either Franklin Jones or Bubba Free John.) This enquiry, which functions as the "arm" of what Da calls "radical understanding," serves to instigate the meditator's return to the state of "plugged-in presence," or relationship, which, in the case of an advanced practitioner, spontaneously morphs into nondual Being-Consciousness, or Mind-as-Thusness. Anyone who can deeply practice Self-enquiry and/or relational enquiry will have no need for nor interest in any other "koans" or enquiries. Hence, "Future Zen," as I envisage it, will emphasize these two practices.

Regarding energy work, because all Rinzai students in Japan are now in Hakuin's lineage, many practice *nikan*, the Taoist alchemical method of drawing energy down the front of the body into the *hara*, and even to one's feet. This method, which involves visualization (Google "Hakuin's soft butter meditation" for descriptions of this practice), seeks to open the frontal line of the body by "pulling-down" *chi* (or *ki*). Although this is a perfectly fine method, it's not on the same level as *Shaktipat* yoga, which seeks to pull down Divine Power, the *Sambhogakaya*. Hence, beyond *nikan*, "Future Zen" would teach students how to directly commune with the *Shakti*, or *Sambhogakaya*, and channel its Blessing Power.

If Zen practice included the dimension of Grace, of consciously opening to and receiving Blessing Power from above, Hakuin and his fellow monks wouldn't have developed energy disorders and needed to resort to the Taoist tradition for a cure. But because Zen doesn't recognize the *Sambhogakaya* as a Body of Grace, equivalent in function to the Christian Holy Spirit and Hindu *Shakti*, its practitioners don't avail themselves of its Blessing (and Healing) Power.

What's the most direct way for Zen practitioners to open to the dimension of Grace and receive Shaktipat, *the down-poured* Sambhogakaya?

My Plugged-in-Presence method, which is akin to Dzogchen *trekcho/togal* and the mystical Eucharist, true Holy Communion. Here [below] are the Instructions from my book *Electrical Christianity*. If a Zennist substitutes "Sambhogakaya" for "Holy Spirit" and "Dharmakaya" for "the Divine," that will make it "Zen."

PLUGGED-IN PRESENCE INSTRUCTIONS

1) Sit upright, but relaxed, on a chair, bench, or meditation cushion.

2) Establish what the Buddha called "self-possession." In other words, feel yourself as the whole body, and then be consciously present as the whole body, the whole psycho-physical being. Randomly focusing your attention on your third-eye area and hands will enable you to coincide with your body, and thereby heal the body-mind split. When you consciously inhabit your whole body—and are wholly, or integrally, present to the whole (the totality of existence)—you are in proper position

to receive and conduct the Holy Spirit, the Force-flow from above.

3) "Gaze" into empty space. If you are "self-possessed," this "gaze" will amount to being whole-bodily present to (or in direct relationship to) the void. As soon as you become aware that you have retracted from your "position" of conscious connectedness to (or single-pointed focus on) the void, simply reassume, or attempt to reassume, your "stance" of holistic at-one-ment. To this end, you can randomly use an enquiry (such as "Avoiding relationship?") to instigate your resumption of communion with the void. When the void begins to "shine," it is experienced as Divine Presence. When the Power of the Presence pours down upon you, then "emptiness" has morphed into Spirit, and your "gaze into space" has transmuted into empowered Divine Communion.

4) Randomly focus your attention on your breath by being in direct relationship to your breathing cycle. When the breath "comes alive" as *prana-shakti*, or palpable intensified life-energy, simply remain present to it. Your communion with the breath cycle will transmute into true, or infused, Divine Communion when the *prana-shakti* morphs into the Holy Spirit— the great *Shakti* poured down from above.

5) Totally relax your body (including your head) and utterly let go of your mind. Once you are able to connect to the *Shakti*, you will directly experience that letting go intensifies the force-flow (or pressure) of the Spirit-current. Be an empty

cup, ready to be filled with Holy Water from above. When you experience the Benediction, the Divine downpour, remain motivelessly present to it. Your searchless beholding of the *Shakti* will enable you to spontaneously merge with it.

These technical meditation instructions are all about facilitating communion, and then union, with the Divine. It is up to you to test them out and determine how useful they are for your spiritual practice. Truly speaking, no spiritual practice, in and of itself, is holy or sacred. The only "Thing" holy or sacred is the Holy One Himself (including His Holy Spirit). Therefore, whatever practices bring you into communion with the Holy One are the ones you should employ.

Electrical Zen, Eclectic Zen

Do you equate "Electrical Zen" with "Future Zen"?

Yes, because my Electrical Spiritual Paradigm (ESP), rightly understood, explains the en-Light-enment process, the turnings of the wheel, and the *Trikaya*. As such, it can be considered a fifth turning of the wheel that elevates Zen to an integral level. And Plugged-in-Presence is the integral practice that enables disciples to directly experience the reality of ESP. I'll now, again, explain why Electrical Buddhism (or Dharma) represents the fifth turning of the wheel.

There have been four turnings of the wheel in Buddhism: 1) The Buddha's original Dharma, 2) Madhyamaka's emptiness Dharma, 3) Yogacara's Mind-only (or Buddha-nature) Dharma, and 4) Vajrayana's tantra Dharma. Because Zen never moved beyond the third turning and is rooted in the second, for it to become "Future Zen" (or "Future Buddhism"), it must incorporate and move beyond the fourth turning by rooting itself in the fifth: "Electrical Dharma," which applies Ohm's Law to explicate the en-Light-enment process, and the Plugged-in Presence method to directly experience it.

For those unfamiliar with Ohm's Law, it states that "the strength or intensity of an unvarying electric current is directly proportional to the electromotive force and inversely proportional to the resistance in a circuit." Ohm's Law—where V = voltage (electromotive force), I = amperage (intensity of current), and R = ohms (units of resistance)—can be summarized in three formulas:

$$V = IR; I = V/R; R = V/I$$

(Note: Any form of the Ohm's Law equation can be derived from the other two via simple algebra.)

All one has to do to translate Ohm's Law into Electrical Dharma is to substitute consciousness-force for voltage, intensity of the Spirit-current for amperage, and reduction of psycho-physical resistance for ohms. And once the disciple awakens the Spirit-current (akin to amperage) and realizes that either intensifying his conscious presence (akin to voltage increase) or decreasing his resistance by letting go (akin to ohms reduction) simultaneously accelerates the force-flow of the Spirit (or Light-Energy)-current, then Electrical Dharma and the en-Light-enment process will make sense to him.

Electrical Buddhism, or Dharma, represents the fifth turning of the wheel because it demystifies the previous turnings and incorporates their essences into a holistic new Buddhadharma. The first turning of the wheel, by Gautama Buddha himself, set the wheel in motion; the second, by Madhyamaka, emphasized Emptiness (Absence, or "Ohms reduction"); the third, by Yogacara, accentuated Mind (Presence, or "Voltage"); and the fourth, by Vajrayana, focused on Energy (Power, or "Current"). Each of the turnings after the Buddha's represents one-third of Ohm's Law, and because Electrical Dharma integrates them into a single whole, it should be considered the fifth turning of the wheel.

So "Future Zen" is simply Electrical Zen?

Yes and no. For Zen to become "Future Zen," it must incorporate "Electrical Dharma." But Zen shouldn't stop there. The term *Zen* derives from *Dhyana*, the Sanskrit word for meditation; so there is no reason why Zen, as a synonym for meditation, can't freely add meditation teachings from other traditions, including non-Buddhist ones. Hence, I predict that in the future, a brilliant, eclectic Zen master will emerge; and after he upgrades Zen, it will not be just "Electrical Zen," but also "Eclectic Zen," for he will integrate the essential teachings of Dzogchen, the mystical Eucharist, Ramana Maharshi, Adi Da, Kashmir Shaivism, the *Yoga Sutras*, et al. into a holistic Dharma that not only exalts the Zen Mind, but also the thinker's mind.

Glossary

Adi-Buddha Samantabhadra: The Primordial *Buddha*. The personification of the *Dharmakaya* that is akin to *Siva* as the personification of the Absolute in Hindu Shaivism.

Advaita Vedanta: The nondual school of Hindu philosophy which asserts that one's True Self (*Atman*) is the same as the Divine Being (*Brahman*).

Ahamkara: Separate-self sense. *Ahamkara* is one of the four parts of the *antahkarana* (inner "organ" of thought, feeling, and memory) described in Vedanta. The other three parts are *buddhi*, *manas*, and *citta*.

Akasha: The ether, or universal space element, wherefrom the four fundamental elements (fire, earth, air, water) derive.

Alaya: The unborn Realm, universal Mind.

Alaya-vijnana: The *Alaya* (universal Consciousness) conjoined with *manas* by *vijnana* in the Heart-center/cave, the *Tathagatagarbha*. A synonym for *citta*, which functions as the "storehouse consciousness," or repository, of one's psychical seed impressions/tendencies (*samskaras*).

Amrita Nadi: The Force (or *Shakti*)-current between the spiritual Heart-center and the crown. The terminal portion/branch of *sushumna nadi*, through which immortal "Nectar," Blessing/Blissing Clear-Light Energy, flows.

Anahata: The subtle-body heart chakra.

Ananda: Bliss—really *Shakti*-Bliss—which stems from the enactment of Being-Consciousness (*Sat-Cit*).

Anandamaya kosha: The Bliss Sheath (or Body). *Shakti* (the *Sambhogakaya*) perceived and enjoyed as separate from *Siva* (the *Dharmakaya*). In *Vedanta*, the fifth of the five sheaths covering (and thus preventing the realization of) the immanent Self (or *Buddha*).

Ananda-Shakti: Divine Blissing Power. The *Sambhogakaya* as the dynamic Bliss Body.

Anatta / Anatman: Not Self.

Annamaya kosha: The sheath composed of food; that is, of material elements: the physical body. In *Vedanta*, the first of the five sheaths covering the Self.

Anugraha-Shakti: Divine Blessing Power, or Grace.

Asana: Psycho-physical "position," "seat," or "stance."

Atiyoga: The highest *tantra* of the Nyingmapa school of Tibetan Buddhism and a synonym for *Dzogchen*. Primordial yoga, meaning the yogic enactment of the Great Perfection.

Atman: A synonym for Self, Christ, and *Buddha*. Immanent *Brahman*.

Bhagavan: A "Blessed One" or Divine personage. Etymologically, *Bhagavan* means penis in the vagina, signifying a being who has united *Siva* and *Shakti*, and thus realized the Self.

Bhumi: Stage or level. Typically used in Mahayana Buddhism to describe the ten stages or levels of spiritual attainment that culminate in *Buddhahood*.

Bhutatathata: The Absolute as the Suchness of all existents.

Bija: Seed. *Bijas* are the karmic "seeds," produced by subconscious psychical impressions (*samskaras*) in the *citta,* or *Alaya-vijnana*. They "sprout" into *vasanas* (habit-energies) when activated.

Bodhi: Enlightenment or Enlightened.

Bodhicitta: Enlightened, or Awakened, Consciousness. *Buddhahood*.

Bodhisattva: An Enlightenment-minded seeker of *Bodhicitta*.

Brahman: Ultimate Reality. The changeless, infinite Divine Being, typically described as *Sat-Cit-Ananda*.

Buddha / Buddha-Nature: A synonym for *Atman*, Self, or Christ. The immanent *Dharmakaya*, or Mind.

Buddhadharma: Buddhist *Dharma*, or Teaching.

Buddhahood: *Bodhicitta*, or *Nirvana*.

Buddhi: The "higher mind." The intellect, or discriminating intelligence of the mind.

Catuskoti: The four-cornered logico-epistemological system of argumentation commonly referred to as the *tetralemma* in Buddhism.

Chakra: Literally a "wheel" or "center." The *chakras* are subtle-body centers where *pranic* channels converge into rotating vortices of energy, which, when blocked, can be likened to "knots," and when open, can produce various "spiritual" phenomena.

Ch'an/Chan: The Chinese term for *Zen*. It derives from the Sanskrit term *dhyana*, which mean "meditation."

Chi/Ki: Etheric life-force energy; equivalent to *prana*.

Cit: Universal, transcendental Consciousness.

Citta: Immanent Consciousness itself (*Cit*) intertwined with *manas* and contracted by grasping (or acts of binding attention) engendered by *vijnana*. When *citta* is permanently de-contracted, it shines as *Cit*, or *Bodhicitta,* and though functioning as *manas* and *vijnana*, it is no longer contracted by them. This is tantamount to the conversion of the *Alaya-vijnana* from an "organ" of bondage and becoming to an "instrument" of Enlightenment.

Cittamatra: A sub-system of *Yogacara* which asserts that a single universal Mind (or Consciousness) has become everything. As such, it is akin to Hindu Kashmir Shaivism and Tibetan *Dzogchen*, which likewise assert that a single omnipresent Consciousness or Awareness (*Siva* or *Dharmakaya*), has manifested as all existents.

Dharma/dharma: When capitalized, spiritual teaching or Truth or Law. When uncapitalized, a conditional thing or phenomenon.

Dharmadhatu: The *Dharmakaya* as the all-pervading, spaceless Substratum underlying phenomenal existence.

Dharmakaya: Universal, timeless Awareness or Consciousness.

Dharmamegha: The "rained-down" descent of the *Dharmakaya* (as the *Sambhogakaya*), which, when "full-blown," "produces" *Bodhicitta*. Sometimes, the term "Great *Dharmamegha*" is used to differentiate "full-blown" *Dharmamegha* from "partial" *Dharmamegha*.

Dharmata: The *Dharmakaya* as universal Suchness, or Beingness. The True Nature of existence. A synonym for *Tathata*.

Dhyana: Meditation. The Sanskrit equivalent of Japanese *Zen* and Chinese *Chan*.

Dzogchen: The Great Perfection. The Tibetan Buddhist and Bon traditions/practices aimed at directly realizing the primordial State of Being.

Guru: Remover of darkness, or ignorance. A Self-realized being who unobstructedly radiates Light.

Hara: The vital center, or "Sea of *Chi*," located just before or directly behind the umbilicus.

Hindudharma: Hindu *Dharma*, or Teaching.

Hridaya/Hridayam: The spiritual Heart. A synonym for the immanent Self and the center, relative to the body, through which it radiates.

Hridaya-granthi: The Heart-knot, which, when severed, results in Self-realization and the "regeneration" of *Amrita Nadi*, which rises from the Heart-center (felt/experienced two digits to the right of center of one's chest) to the Crown and beyond.

Hridaya-Shakti: The radiant *Shakti* emitted from/through the Heart-center of an Enlightened being. A synonym for the *Nirmanakaya* in standard Dzogchen teachings. [Note: my definition of *Nirmanakaya* does not equate it with *Hridaya-Shakti*.]

Jhana: Meditative state of engrossment. The Four *Jhanas*, which constitute the eighth limb (Right Contemplation) of the Buddha's Noble Eightfold path, are progressive states of absorption in the Stream, or Spirit-current. In yogic terminology, they equate to *samadhis*.

Jnani: A yogi who practices or who has achieved mastery in Jnana yoga, the yoga of Self-knowledge.

Kaivalya: Isolation, meaning exclusive realization of, or absorption in, the Self, or *Buddha*, sans defiling taints.

Klesa: Affliction or defilement.

Klista-manas: The seventh consciousness (of eight) in *Yogacara*. The taint-ridden, self-grasping mind, which is akin to the Sanskrit term *ahamkara* (egoic self-sense).

Koan: Confounding, paradoxical question that, in Zen, serves as an object of meditation.

Kosha: Sheath, or covering.

Kundalini/Kundalini-Shakti: The "Serpent Power." The dynamic force-flow of "uncoiled" energy that accompanies spiritual awakening. The so-called "higher *Kundalini*" refers to *Shaktipat*, the descent of Divine Power.

Madhyamaka: A school of Mahayana Buddhism, systematized by Nagarjuna, which emphasizes the emptiness of all phenomena.

Mahamudra: The Great Seal, Symbol, and Gesture. And the "Great Gesture," or yogic "Holo-Act," is uniting the son light (the *nirmanakaya*) with the Mother Light (the *Sambhogakaya*), which yields realization of the Father (the *Dharmakaya*).

Manas: The mind that processes and mediates sensory information and habit-tendencies (*vasanas*). The mind in general.

Manomaya kosha: The sheath of mind. In *Vedanta*, the third of the five sheaths covering the Self.

Mano-vijnana: The sixth consciousness (of eight) in *Yogacara*. The mental consciousness that cognitively processes sense-data and engages in concept formation.

Maya: That which has been measured out from the Immeasurable. Phenomenal existence or reality.

Mother Shakti: *Shakti* personified as the Divine Mother or Goddess.

Nadis: Energy channels in the body. These include the subtle-body channels through which *prana* and *Kundalini* flow and, in the case of *Amrita Nadi*, the causal-body channel through which immortal "Nectar," Blessing/Blissing Clear-Light Energy, streams.

Neti-Neti: "Not this, not this." The meditation practice of dis-identifying from all that is not one's Self, or *Buddha-nature*.

Nikan: The Taoist alchemical method of drawing energy down the front of the body into the *hara*, and even to one's feet.

Nirmanakaya: The immanent *Dharmakaya*. The Enlightened form body, or manifest *Buddha*. Akin to the Christian Son, or Christ.

Nirvana: The end of becoming (*samsara*), which signifies Blissful (Divine) Being. Equivalent to Hindu *Sat-Cit-Ananda*.

Panca-skandha: The Five Aggregates (or Grasping Groups) in Buddhism: Rupa: form, matter, or body; Vedana: sensations resulting from contact with rupa; Samjna: perception, meaning awareness and integration of sensations; Sankhara: mental formations, conditioning, and imprints; *Vijnana*: consciousness functioning as discriminating intelligence.

Pandit: *Dharma* scholar/teacher.

Pneumatic: An individual awake to the Spirit.

Prana: Etheric life-force energy. Equivalent to *chi*.

Pranamaya kosha: The sheath composed of life-force: the etheric body in Western occult literature. In *Vedanta*, the second of five sheaths covering the Self.

Pranayama: Conscious breathing exercise(s) aimed at balancing and/or intensifying the flow of *prana* through one's subtle-body *nadis*.

Prasangika-Madhyamaka: Subdivision of *Madhyamaka* that emphasizes the ultimate truth of emptiness beyond all conceptual elaboration.

Pratityasamutpada: Dependent origination: the twelve-fold chain of links in Buddhist teachings describing the causal arising of mental formations and suffering.

Rigpa: The *Dzogchen* practice of primal presence, which bestows radical (or gone-to-the-root) gnosis (or spiritual knowledge) and whole-body en-Light-enment (or Spirit-current irradiation). It is commonly described as naked or intrinsic awareness, but because one is being, or attempting to be, present *as* this awareness, it is better described as direct and immediate presence.

Rinzai: A sect and style of *Zen* that is somewhat martial in nature compared to *Soto*, the other major *Zen* sect. *Rinzai* stresses *koans*, whereas *Soto* emphasizes *shikantaza*, the more passive "nothing but sitting."

Samadhi: A state of meditative absorption or unbroken spiritual contemplation.

Samantabhadra: The primordial *Buddha*, a.k.a. *Adi-Buddha*, who is akin to *Siva* in tantric Shaivism.

Sambhogakaya: The Bliss, or Light, Body. The *Dharmakaya* as Blessing/Blissing Clear-Light Energy. Equivalent to Hindu *Shakti* and the Christian Holy Spirit/Ghost.

Samsara: The cycle of birth and death. "Becoming," the succession of limited and unsatisfactory states of being.

Samskaras: Subconscious psychical impressions in the *citta*, or *Alaya-vijnana*, which, when activated, concatenate into *vasanas,* desire-impulses, or habit-energies.

Sat-Cit-Ananda: Being-Consciousness-Bliss.

Satori: Japanese term for the experience of *kensho* (seeing into one's True Nature).

Satsang: Fellowship with Being. The term is usually associated with the practice of Divine Communion in the context of a spiritual group; but one does not need the presence of a group or a *guru* to practice *Satsang*.

Semde: The Mind Division (or Series), which is one of three scriptural divisions in *Dzogchen*: Semde (Mind), Longde (Space), and Menngagde (Secret or Instruction). Semde emphasizes the practice of presence; Longde focuses on empty space in relation to the Natural State; and Menngagde pertains to *trekcho* and *togal* teachings.

Shakti: Divine Power, or Clear-Light Energy. Equivalent to the Buddhist *Sambhogakaya* and the Christian Holy Spirit.

Shaktipat: The descent of Divine Power (or Grace), which can occur spontaneously in a disciple or be instigated by a spiritual master.

Shikantaza: "Nothing but sitting." The *Rinzai* "practice" of "no-practice," meaning purposeless, objectless awareness.

Siva: The personification of the Absolute in Hindu Shaivism. Akin to the *Adi-Buddha*, or *Samantabhadra*, in *Vajrayana* Buddhism.

Siva-Shakti: The Absolute (or Divine Being) depicted as Consciousness-Power rather than just Consciousness (*Siva*).

Skandha: Aggregate, heap, or mass. In Buddhism, the five *skandhas*, or factors that constitute an individual, are: Rupa: form, matter, or body; Vedana: sensations resulting from contact with rupa; Samjna: perception, meaning awareness and integration of sensations; Sankhara: mental formations, conditioning, and imprints; *Vijnana*: consciousness functioning as discriminating intelligence.

Sotapatti: The stage of entering the Stream in Pali Buddhism. Akin to baptism in/by the Spirit in Christianity.

Soto: A sect and style of *Zen* that is passive in nature compared to *Rinzai*, the other major Zen sect. *Soto* emphasizes *shikantaza*, "nothing but sitting," whereas *Rinzai* stresses forceful *koan* practice.

Sunyata: Emptiness or voidness.

Sushumna: The central yogic channel (*nadi*) through which *Kundalini* moves.

Sutra/Sutta: "Thread" or scripture.

Svabhava: Void of self-essence or intrinsic nature.

Tantra: Derives from "tan," which means to weave and expand. A *tantric* yogi weaves the strands of his nature into a unified whole, which frees and "expands" (or de-contracts) his consciousness. Spiritual alchemy: the transubstantiation of one's entire being into single, radiant Intensity.

Tathagata: A *Buddha*, or "thus-gone one," who unbrokenly and irreversibly abides in Thusness, or Suchness, or Beingness.

Tathagatagarbha: The "womb" or matrix where a *Buddha*, or "Thus-Gone One," is "reborn," or Awakened. Akin to the "cave of the Heart" in Hinduism.

Tathata: Thusness, Suchness, or Beingness. A synonym for *Dharmata*.

Tetralemma: The four-cornered logico-epistemological system of argumentation commonly employed by *Madhyamaka* proponents.

Thigle: A luminous sphere or drop of "rainbow light" that is a manifestation of the Clear Light.

Togal: "Leap-Over" or "Direct Crossing." Directly contacting Spirit, the *Sambhogakaya*, or "Other Side," and contemplating/conducting its Clear-Light Energy. The "conductivity" aspect of *rigpa*, wherein the yogi experiences four progressive states, or "visions," of Enlightenment that culminate in the realization of *Dharmata*, the *Dharmakaya* as universal Suchness, or Beingness.

Trekcho: "Breakthrough." The implementation of one's consciousness as a "cutting tool" to break through to the "Other Side," which is Spirit, or the *Sambhogakaya*. One's consciousness is transformed into such a cutting tool by one assuming, and maintaining, the *asana*, or "position," of direct, immediate presence. Hence, *trekcho* is simply *rigpa* applied as a "cutting tool."

Trikaya: The Buddhist Triple Body (*Dharmakaya*, *Sambhogakaya*, *Nirmanakaya*). The *Dharmakaya* viewed three-dimensionally as: transcendental, universal Consciousness; Blessing/ Blissing Clear-Light Energy; and immanent, embodied Consciousness.

Vajrayana: "Diamond Vehicle" tantric Buddhism, which seeks to "cut through" obstacles to Enlightenment by alchemically integrating and transcending them.

Vasana: Habit-energy or desire-impulse.

Vedanta: This term literally means "end of the Vedas." It is an umbrella term for the many sub-traditions, ranging from dualism to nondualism, that have a common connection to the *Principal Upanishads*, the *Brahma Sutras*, and the *Bhagavad Gita*.

Vijnana: This term has two meanings: 1) consciousness functioning as discriminating intelligence, meaning the "higher mind," and 2) consciousness functioning dualistically.

Vijnamaya kosha: The sheath composed of understanding and discrimination. The "lower mind" coordinates sensory input and general mental activity, but understanding (*vijnana*) is a higher cognitive function. In *Vedanta*, the fourth of five sheaths covering the Self.

Vijnaptimatra: The *Yogacara* "mind-only" school, which asserts that the world is nothing but ideas, with no Reality or realities behind them, and that all *dharmas* (or things) are mere mental projections, or cognitions, or representations, of one's individual mind.

Yogacara: The Mahayana Buddhist "Mind-Only" school, which consists of two distinct subschools: *Vijnaptimatra* (which asserts that all things are mere mental projections), and *Cittamatra* (which views all things as manifestations of universal Mind).

Zen: The term *Zen* (*Ch'an* in Chinese) derives from *dhyana* (Sanskrit), which means meditation. Hence, Zen Buddhism is Buddhism which emphasizes meditation while deemphasizing other aspects of *Buddhadharma*.

Spiritual Reading List

Advaita Vedanta

Highly Recommended

Ashtavakra Gita, trans. Hari Prasad Shastri. (Timeless Advaita Vedanta text. Available at www.shantisadan.org. Other translations also available.)

Be As You Are: The Teachings of Ramana Maharshi, David Godman. (Best introductory book on the teachings of Ramana Maharshi.)

Sat-Darshana Bhashya and Talks with Maharshi, Sri Ramanasramam. (A learned devotee's in-depth consideration of Ramana Maharshi's teachings within the framework of Indian-yogic philosophy.)

Sri Ramana Gita, Ramana Maharshi. (An utterly unique, ultra-profound text that details the function of the Amrita Nadi in the Self-realization process.)

Talks with Sri Ramana Maharshi, Ramana Maharshi. (Must-reading. A truly great and inspiring book. Avoid the dumbed-down version published by Inner Directions.)

(*Sat-Darshana Bhashya, Sri Ramana Gita,* and *Talks with Sri Ramana Maharshi* are available at www.arunachala.org.)

Recommended

Be Who You Are (or any of Jean Klein's books), Jean Klein.

I Am That: Talks with Sri Nisargadatta Maharaj, Maurice Frydman. (Classic, über-popular text.)

Silence of the Heart, Robert Adams.

Vivekachudamani (Crest Jewel of Discrimination), trans. Swami Prabhavananda and Christopher Isherwood. (Other translations of Shankara's teachings also available.)

Who Am I? Meditation, Ramaji. (If you like this text, get his *The Spiritual Heart.*)

Buddhism (Original)

<u>Highly Recommended</u>

Some Sayings of the Buddha: According to the Pali Canon, F.L. Woodward. (Easily the finest presentation of the Buddha's core teachings.)

The Wings to Awakening: An Anthology from the Pali Canon, Thanissaro Bhikku. (Outstanding translation of and commentary on the Buddha's essential meditation teachings. Free download available on the Internet.)

<u>Recommended</u>

Buddhism: An Outline of its Teachings and Schools, Hans Wolfgang Schuman. (Solid academic book.)

In the Buddha's Words: An Anthology of Discourses from the Pali Canon, Bhikku Bodhi. (Comprehensive introduction to the Buddha's teachings.)

Mindfulness in Plain English, Venerable Henepola Gunaratana. (Basic introductory text on insight meditation.)

The Doctrine of Awakening: The Attainment of Self-Mastery According to the Earliest Buddhist Texts, Julius Evola (Unique consideration of Pali Buddhism.)

The Heart of Buddhist Meditation, Nyaponika Thera. (Classic text on insight meditation.)

The Living Thoughts of Gotama the Buddha, Ananda Coomaraswamy and I.B. Horner. (Classic text. Excellent introduction to Buddhism.)

The Way of Non-Attachment, Dhiravamsa. (Unique Krishnamurti-influenced book on insight meditation. Out of print.)

Buddhism (Tibetan)

<u>Highly Recommended</u>

Principal Yogacara Texts: Indo-Tibetan Sources of Dzogchen Mahamudra, Rodney P. Devenish. (Easily the best Yogacara text I've encountered.)

Teachings of Tibetan Yoga, Garma C.C. Chang. (Superb Mahamudra presentation. Must- reading for serious meditators.)

The Cycle of Day and Night, Namkhai Norbu. (Outstanding Dzogchen meditation manual. Must- reading for serious meditators.)

The Golden Letters, John Myrdhin Reynolds. (Scholarly exposition of the history and practice of Dzogchen in relation to the Garab Dorje, the first teacher of Dzogchen.)

The Precious Treasury of the Way of Abiding, Longchen Rabjam. (Marvelous ultra-mystical text by a revered Vajrayana master. If you appreciate this book, get *A Treasure Trove of Scriptural Transmission: A Commentary on The Precious Treasury of the Basic Space of Phenomena*, by the same author. Other translations/annotations of Rabjam's texts are available.)

Recommended

Cutting Through Spiritual Materialism, Chogyam Trungpa. (Enlightening text by a modern "crazy wisdom" master.)

Naked Awareness, Karma Chagme. (Excellent material on Dzogchen and Mahamudra.)

Self-Liberation Though Seeing with Naked Awareness, John Myrdhin Reynolds. (Compare this translation of/commentary on Padmasambhava's *Yoga of Knowing the Mind and Seeing Reality* to W.Y. Evans-Wentz's in The Tibetan Book of the Great Liberation.)

The Supreme Source, Namkhai Norbu. (The fundamental tantric text of Dzogchen.)

The Tibetan Book of the Great Liberation, W.Y. Evans-Wentz. (Classic translation of/commentary on Padmasambhava's *Yoga of Knowing the Mind and Seeing Reality*. Compare this translation/commentary to John Myrdhin Reynolds's in Self-Liberation Through Seeing with Naked Awareness. Skip Carl Jung's ridiculous "Psychological Commentary.")

Tibetan Yoga and Secret Doctrines, W.Y. Evans-Wentz. (Classic, ultra-mystical text.)

Wonders of the Natural Mind, Tenzin Wangyal. (The essence of Dzogchen in the Native Bon Tradition of Tibet.)

(Although I have little good to say about Longchen Rabjam's *Precious Treasury of the Genuine Meaning*, it's must-reading for those interested in standard Dzogchen *togal*, as is Jigme Lingpa's *Yeshe Lama*, another text I hold in low regard. Sam van Schaik's *Approaching the*

Great Perfection: Simultaneous and Gradual Methods of Dzogchen Practice in the Longchen Nyingtig and *Naked Seeing: The Great Perfection, the Wheel of Time and Visionary Buddhism in Renaissance Tibet* by Christopher Hatchell are interesting, information-packed academic texts that serious students of *togal* will appreciate.)

Buddhism (Zen)

<u>Highly Recommended</u>

The Diamond Sutra and the Sutra of Hui Neng, trans. A.F. Price. (Other translations of these timeless sutras also available.)

Tracing Back the Radiance: Chinul's Korean Way of Zen, Robert Buswell, Jr. (Outstanding account of a great Zen master's spiritual evolution.)

The Zen Teaching of Huang Po, John Blofeld. (Easily the best book on Zen.)

<u>Recommended</u>

Kensho, The Heart of Zen, Thomas Cleary. (My favorite Cleary text on Zen.)

Practical Zen: Meditation and Beyond, Julian Daizan Skinner. (Excellent beginner-intermediate Zen instruction text.)

The Lankavatara Sutra, trans. D.T. Suzuki. (Avoid Red Pine's "butchered" translation.)

The Practice of Zen, Garma C.C. Chang. (Great autobiographical accounts of enlightenment. (Out of print.)

The Rinzai Zen Way: A Guide to Practice, Meido Moore. (Excellent beginner-intermediate Zen instruction text.)

The Three Pillars of Zen, Philip Kapleau. (Classic, popular Rinzai Zen text that emphasizes the satori experience.)

The Way of Zen, Alan Watts. (Classic introductory text by the godfather of American Zen.)

Zen Mind, Beginner's Mind, Shunryu Suzuki. (Classic, ultra-popular Soto Zen text.)

Zen Teaching of Instantaneous Awakening, Ch'an Master Hui Hai; trans. John Blofeld. (Fine Dharma instructions by a great Chinese Ch'an master.)

(Scholarly types will enjoy Heinrich Dumoulin's *Zen Buddhism: A History (India and China)* and *Zen Buddhism: A History (Japan), Vol. 2.* Serious students of Buddhist philosophy will appreciate Garma C.C. Chang's *The Buddhist Teaching of Totality*, which expounds Hwa Yen Buddhism's all-embracing philosophy in relation to Zen. If you enjoy reading Zen, check out Thomas Cleary's numerous books at Amazon.com. Edward Conze's *Selected Sayings from the Perfection of Wisdom* is a fine anthology of sayings from the Prajnaparamita Sutras, including the *Heart Sutra*.)

Christianity, Judaism, and Gnosticism

Highly Recommended

Meditations on the Tarot, Valentin Tomberg. (An astonishing journey into Christian Hermeticism. Must-reading for anyone interested in Christian mysticism.)

Meister Eckhart. (*The Complete Mystical Works of Meister Eckhart* is the book I recommend—but it costs $98. *Meister Eckhart*, trans. Raymond B. Blakney, is a fine compilation of Eckhart's sermons, and goes for about $15. Scholarly types will want to supplement either of the aforementioned books with *The Mystical Thought of Meister Eckhart* by Bernard McGinn.)

Mysticism, Evelyn Underwood. (Wonderful, classic, early twentieth-century text by the first lady of Christian mysticism.)

The Foundations of Mysticism. Bernard McGinn. (Extraordinary presentation of the Western mystical tradition. Must-reading for scholarly types.)

Recommended

Inner Christianity, Richard Smoley. (Clear and thoughtful guide to the esoteric Christian tradition.)

Jesus Christ, Sun of God, David Fideler (Fascinating read on ancient cosmology, gnostic symbolism, Pythagorean number theory, and Hellenistic gematria.)

Jewish Meditation, Aryeh Kaplan.

Open Mind, Open Heart, Thomas Keating. (Classic, best-selling text on the Gospel's contemplative dimension.)

The Big Book of Christian Mysticism: The Essential Guide to Contemplative Spirituality, Carl McColman. (Good introductory text and resource guide for those interested in Christian mysticism.)

The Mystic Christ, Ethan Walker. (Excellent book for Christians.)

The Practice of the Presence of God, Brother Lawrence, Robert Edmondson, and Jonathon Wilson-Hartgrove. (Classic text on the practice of establishing a conscious relationship with the Divine.)

The Secret Book of John, trans. Stevan Davies.

The Sermon on the Mount According to Vedanta, Swami Prabhavananda.

The Way of a Pilgrim and the Pilgrim Continues His Way, Multiple fine translations available. (Inspiring book for practitioners of prayer and mantra meditation.)

(Scholarly types into Western Christian mysticism will love all the fine texts by Prof. Bernard McGinn. Check out his seven-volume *The Presence of God Series*, which, begins with the highly recommended *The Foundations of Mysticism*. Beyond this series, McGinn has graced us with *The Essential Writings of Christian Mysticism*, an immensely rich anthology of the greatest Christian mystical literature. Selections in this volume include writings from such great mystics as Origen, Augustine, Pseudo-Dionysius the Areopagite, St. John of the Cross, Bernard of Clairvaux, Meister Eckhart, John Ruysbroeck, and many more. For a scholarly consideration of Jewish mysticism, I recommend Gershom Scholem's *Major Trends in Jewish Mysticism and Moshe Idel's Kabbalah: New Perspectives*. Scholem's text is the canonical modern work on the nature and history of Jewish mysticism, while Idel's is the foremost scholarly consideration of Kabbalah.)

Daism

<u>Highly Recommended</u>

Hridaya Rosary (Four Thorns of Heart-Instruction), Adi Da Samraj. (Excellent technical devotional-meditation book.)

The Knee of Listening, Adi Da Samraj. (Best spiritual autobiography ever written. Must-reading for mystics. Get a copy of the latest edition, but also get a copy of an earlier edition written under either the names of Franklin Jones or Bubba Free John. These earlier editions, unlike later and current editions, contain Da's outstanding "Meditation of Understanding," instructions on the practice of "real meditation," or "radical understanding.")

The Liberator: The "Radical" Reality-Teachings of The Great Avataric Sage, Adi Da Samraj, Adi Da Samraj.

The Method of the Siddhas, Adi Da Samraj. (A truly great spiritual book. Out of print and only available used. Try to get a copy written under the name of either Franklin Jones or Bubba Free John. The current revised edition of the book, entitled *My "Bright" Word*, lacks the direct visceral impact of the original text.)

The Pneumaton, Adi Da Samraj. (Ultra-esoteric consideration of "Pneuma," the Spirit.)

The Way of Perfect Knowledge: The "Radical" Practice of Transcendental Spirituality in the Way of Adidam, Adi Da Samraj.

Recommended

He-And-She Is Me: The Indivisibility of Consciousness and Light In the Divine Body of the Ruchira Avatar, Adi Da Samraj.

Ruchira Avatara Hridaya-Siddha Yoga: The Divine (and Not Merely Cosmic) Spiritual Baptism in the Way of Adidam, Adi Da Samraj.

Santosha Adidam: The Essential Summary of the Divine Way of Adidam, Adi Da Samraj.

The All-Completing and Final Divine Revelation to Mankind: A Summary Description Of The Supreme Yoga Of The Seventh Stage Of Life In The Divine Way Of Adidam, Adi Da Samraj.

(The four books on the Recommended List contain a number of the same essays. Nonetheless, each book includes enough unique material to merit its reading.)

Hinduism (Yoga)

<u>Highly Recommended</u>

The Bhagavad Gita, translations by Eknath Easwaran, Swami Prabhavananda and Christopher Isherwood, S. Radakrishnan. (Many other fine translations/annotations also available.)

The Yoga of Spiritual Devotion: A Modern Translation of the Narada Bhakti Sutras, Prem Prakesh. (A simple, inspiring text on the spiritual path of love and devotion.)

The Yoga Sutras of Patanjali, Edwin F. Bryant. (A 600-page tome that provides a wealth of information on the history, philosophy, and practice of classical yoga. Serious students of yoga will want to read this text as well as Swami Hariharananda Aranya's *Yoga Philosophy of Patanjali*.)

Yoga Philosophy of Patanjali, Swami Hariharananda Aranya. (A unique and profound account of classical yoga by a scholar-monk.)

<u>Recommended</u>

Be Here Now, Baba Ram Dass. (Classic introductory book on Eastern philosophy. An easy and entertaining read.)

How to Know God, Prabhavananda and Isherwood. (Best introduction to the yoga philosophy of Patanjali.)

The Essential Swami Ramdas, Swami Ramdas. (Inspiring writings of a great twentieth-century *bhakti* yogi.)

The Gospel of Sri Ramakrishna, Swami Nikhilananda. (A revered *bhakti* classic.)

The Synthesis of Yoga, Sri Aurobindo. (Profound essays on yoga by Sri Aurobindo, the renowned twentieth-century Indian guru-philosopher. If you appreciate this book and crave more Aurobindo, get a copy of *The Life Divine*.)

The Upanishads, translations by Mascara, and by Prabhavananda and Isherwood. (Other fine translations also available.)

The Yoga Tradition, Georg Feuerstein. (Outstanding reference book on the history, literature, philosophy, and practice of yoga.)

Kashmir Shaivism

Highly Recommended

Pratyabhijnahrdayam:The Secret of Self-Recognition, Jaideva Singh. (The basic introductory handbook to the abstruse philosophical system of recognition. Not for the intellectually challenged. *The Doctrine of Recognition*, out of print but available as an ebook, is, thanks to the editing of Paul Muller-Ortega, the best version of this text.)

Siva Sutras:The Yoga of Supreme Identity, Jaideva Singh. (The foundational text of Kashmir Shaivism.)

The Doctrine of Vibration, Mark S.G. Dyczkowski. (A scholarly analysis of the doctrines and practices of Kashmir Shaivism.)

The Philosophy of Sadhana, Deba Brata SenSharma. (Outstanding text that deals clearly and extensively with the ultra-important topic of *Shaktipat*, the Descent of Divine Power, or Grace. Must-reading for serious mystics.)

The Triadic Heart of Siva, Paul Eduardo Muller-Ortega. (An ultra-esoteric text about the Heart (*Hridaya*) as Ultimate Reality, Emissional Power, and Embodied Cosmos.)

Recommended

Kundalini, The Energy of the Depths, Lilian Silburn. (As an Amazon.com reviewer puts it, "The foremost modern exposition of *Kundalini*.")

Spanda Karikas: The Divine Creative Pulsation, Jaideva Singh. (An elaboration of the dynamic aspect of Transcendental Consciousness.)

Miscellaneous

Highly Recommended

The First and Last Freedom, J. Krishnamurti. (Must-reading for all mystics. If you appreciate this book and want to read more Krishnamurti, get his multivolume *Commentaries on Living*.)

Introduction to Objectivist Epistemology, Ayn Rand. (Must-reading for all mystics.)

Objectivism: The Philosophy of Ayn Rand, Leonard Peikoff. (Must-reading for all mystics.)

The Way of Chuang Tzu, Thomas Merton. (Other translations also available.)

Recommended

A Brief History of Everything, Ken Wilber. (Wilber, perhaps the most overrated living philosopher, is still worth a read. If you appreciate his pseudo-wisdom, get *Sex, Ecology, Spirituality: The Spirit of Evolution*.)

Alan Oken's Complete Astrology, Alan Oken. (Best overall book on astrology.)

Ayurveda: The Science of Self-Healing, Vasant Lad. (Fascinating and enlightening exposition of the principles and practical applications of Indian Ayurveda, the oldest healing system in the world.)

Awaken Healing Energy Through the Tao, Mantak Chia. (Classic introductory handbook to the practice and principles of Taoist energy yoga.)

The Mystique of Enlightenment: The Radical Ideas of U.G. Krishnamurti, U.G. Krishnmurti (U.G. was the ultimate spiritual iconoclast. Jean Klein called him "pathological." I call him "a great read.")

The Perennial Philosophy, Aldous Huxley. (Classic text by a great writer.)

The Tao Te Ching. (Numerous translations available.)